All you need is cake!

PUBLISHED BY

YOUR UNIQUE DAY

4 GOOSE GATE, HOCKLEY

NOTTINGHAM.

ENGLAND U.K

ISBN NUMBER 978-0-9576378-0-1

ALL YOU NEED IS CAKE ©2012. DANIELLE C.K GOTHERIDGE

SECOND EDITION

PUBLISHER

YOUR UNIQUE DAY

AUTHOR

DANIELLE C.K GOTHERIDGE BA (HONS) FINE ART

EDITORS

ELLA J. GREENWOOD &

ROBYN B. LYDON

PHOTOGRAPHER

AMY MCASKELL

GRAPHIC DESIGNER

PHIL LOWTHER

WWW.DANIELLEGOTHERIDGE.COM

—— Contents ——

— Aim and Introduction —

My aim for this book is to teach several of my secret techniques that are the key to many of my signature designs. Because I started on a very low budget, a lot of my techniques are created using things you find around the house as tools....I want to show how planning your design enables you to open your mind to 'imaginative creating', instead of regimented traditional sugar-craft techniques with old fashioned tools. If you use the same tools as everyone else you're all making the same product! In my book I will give advice on creating your design sheet by gathering information on your 'theme' or 'occasion' and then how to break down the design and work out how to then create it out of icing and cake, what strength of icing you'll need and what type of objects you can use to achieve the designs. If you understand how the materials work, your confidence in using them will grow and grow ....and that's what I aim to do for you!

Every cake book is the same, recipes, covering, then decorations....there is no designing, there's no originality, there's no 'wow factor'. Most of us know how to bake a sponge and make buttercream, and then copy a design of a novelty birthday cake from a book, but how many people know how to create their own completely original designs from scratch?

This book will start at the beginning of the design process, show you how to prepare your cakes, tell you how to stack them and why, then step by step I will show you techniques which are guaranteed to wow an audience every time. You are the designer and this book is simply the guide enabling you to design and create 'wow factor' cakes and amaze anyone who is presented with them.

The 'cupcake course' section at the back of this book also brings something new to cupcake decorating.... discussing themes and creating 'designer' cupcakes as perfect gifts for all occasions. This isn't simply applying some coloured buttercream and punching out a butterfly on top, this is professional decorating on a cupcake scale, and again, incorporating my signature techniques.

You can design and make a cake for all different kinds of celebrations; birthdays, anniversaries, christenings, weddings, etc; this book will be truly useful to assist you in designing that something special for every occasion.

— *My History* —

I was born and brought up within our family pubs and restaurants which were owned by my grandparents, Arthur and Kathleen Gotheridge. This made it easy for me to obtain bar and kitchen work while still studying later on at University. My grandparents also brought me up from the age of 9 months, due to my mother being killed in a car accident. I was always a bright child, but became easily distracted during comprehensive school, just concentrating on the subjects I enjoyed, art and maths. My passion for art, and being creative, took me on my journey through 6 years of college and university.

Between the 2nd and 3rd year of my degree, I fell in love, got married, and a year later at my graduation, we discovered we were expecting our first child Robyn. Because of my upbringing I wanted to be a full time mum and not miss out on a single second, so I decided to put children before my career, despite leaving University with excellent references. After Robyn, came Angel and Casey, my world was complete. I started to produce my children's birthday cakes as I felt supermarket cakes were full of preservatives and my children's diets were extremely important to me. Friends started asking me to do their cakes and seems as I'd had no decorating experience, each design was completely experimental. Everyone was more than happy with the results and word got around. My best friend, who I grew up with, was getting married and my daughters were bridesmaids. I offered to do her wedding cake as her present from me, (as I was dying to have a go at something more challenging). Amy gave me artistic licence to create whatever I liked, I flicked through a couple of cake magazines, but nothing inspired me. I sat at home and started to sketch. I knew the colour scheme from my daughter's dresses and incorporated it into the design. The end result was quite unusual at the time but it was the talking point at the reception. The evening consisted of people telling me I should do it as a career.

The following year my husband announced he was leaving us for another woman. After 10 years, the fairytale was over and the nightmare of supporting 3 children alone began. Amy had began photographing friend's weddings so we decided to go into business together, calling ourselves "Your Unique Day". Amy's husband Ben built us a website and we started exhibiting at wedding fayres. Within 3 months the main wedding venues in Nottingham started promoting us, but after Amy had her 3rd child, she decided to take some time out and I continued the business alone. I carried on designing and creating cakes from home, holding consultations within my house. I would sit and listen

to their plans, themes, colour schemes, personalities and design their cakes in front of them. 100% of the visitors were so impressed with the designs that they went ahead and booked straight away. I enjoyed being creative again and using my knowledge of art history and design to create Unique cakes. My clients started calling my business 'Unique' and that name stuck for the next 4 years.

My eldest daughter, Robyn, was extremely bright and her primary school recommended that she should attend private school, as the next step in her education. Her father refused to help so I decided to open a shop. The shop was small and on a main road, but only 5 minutes from my house and 10 minutes from the children's school, and most importantly, very cheap!

18 months after the shop was opened, I received an email from the main shopping centre in Nottingham. I was shocked and excited that the largest shopping

centre in the city had chosen me out of 8 cake companies, to open an outlet of my business in the busiest location within their centre, based on my designs. My clever daughter built me a new website and of course, my business progressed to a whole new level. Now my designs were being viewed by a much wider audience, shoppers and tourists from all over the world. The response was amazing, and the 'wows' from people walking through the centre was over whelming. After a year I decided to close both outlets and open a city centre shop, in which everything could be produced from one place. My vision from the beginning was always 'Hockley' - a quirky, Bohemian area of Nottingham with independent and individual shops. Quality time with my children was far more important than a chain of shopping centre stalls and I wanted to concentrate on my unique designs rather than a commercial brand. I was also able to reduce my staff of 7 down to my original crew of me and my friend Deborah (a previous fashion student).

At the new shop we have 7 rooms over 4 floors, so after creating our quirky cake gallery on the shop floor, we expanded to a consultation room, 2 kitchens and a course room. Although I'd never had a cake decorating lesson in my life, amateur and professional decorators were booking on my courses to learn my techniques. When the children were young, I had given voluntary art lessons at their school. This was extremely useful when conducting the courses and they soon adapted to educational parties for children too. I love the idea of children having 'educational fun' and teaching them a creative life skill. The response I get from the courses has definitely encouraged me to put the book together, along with the public's response to my shop.

My shop is now called Danielle Gotheridge, out of respect for my grandparents who brought me up to be the strong, independent and business minded person I am today.

— *Design Guide* —

When I was 17 years old, studying for my Art and Design Diploma at the Charnwood Centre (part of South Notts College), I learned the importance of designing my artwork before making it. Since then and with every cake I have made so far, I have stuck to this principle. The design process is just as significant as physically creating the cake.

Subject

First of all ask yourself; who is your cake for? What's the occasion? How many people does it need to feed? You need to decide on the size and structure of the cake before you start designing any of the decoration and asking yourself these questions will help. For example, if it is for a corporate launch party with 200 guests, you might want to go for a large tiered cake to indicate 'grandeur', or if it's a cake for your daughter's 10th birthday party, where there will be 15 guests, a smaller one tiered cake would be more appropriate. Once you have decided on the size and structure, draw a small basic outline of your cake and label it with the measurements. Also add labels showing what type of cake you will be using, if you are designing a tiered cake this is important for the construction [see 'Stacking' page 26-27].

At the top of your design sheet, write down your 'subject' or a title, this way you can keep referring back to it. Make some notes around your subject/title of things that relate to them/it, you should want your cake to be as unique and personal as possible! If it is for an individual, think about what they like, what are their favourite colours, do they have any hobbies? For example, 'Emily': girly, pretty, pink, sparkly, shopping, shoes! 'The Royal Ballet School': classical, uniformed, elegant, logo, spectacular!

Theme

Does the occasion you are designing the cake for have a particular theme? A Halloween party, a masquerade ball, a garden wedding party, a princess-themed birthday party, whatever the theme, start to add to your notes ideas on how to represent it through your cake. For example, ghosts, spiders and witches for Halloween and tea cups, butterflies and flowers for a garden party or wedding. Remember to always keep your subject in mind, for example, 'The Royal Ballet School' may not appreciate a neon yellow tutu cake, even though it represents the theme of ballet, they are more likely to prefer being represented by a delicate ballerina or a theatrical red curtain.

On your design sheet, start to sketch as many things that relate to your theme and subject as possible. The more you do the better.

TIP: If you are struggling for ideas, use the internet. Type your theme into a search engine and see what comes up that inspires you. Maybe visit a place or have a walk round an area that is associated with your theme, take some photos, or sit and sketch a few ideas.

Once you have your 'subject' notes at the top of your page, the size and structure of your cake and plenty of images/drawings indicating your theme, it is now time to focus on your 'points of interest'.

Points of Interest

Think about what images/drawings really emphasise and illustrate your theme. At college we would use a 'view finder', a small square cut out of a piece of paper or card, to look through, moving it over our images/drawings to see what particular parts stood out. For example, the frills on a tutu represent ballet more subtlety, without having to create a whole ballerina. Have fun going over all of your images/drawings with the viewfinder, some of them you might want to keep whole, but for those that you want to section down, think about how to display them on a larger scale for your final cake design. With the tutu frills, you could have them over half of, or a full tier or maybe even all over the cake on each tier.

Incorporating your 'points of interest' into your cake design well will create a unique edible sculpture, a cake with 'wow factor', suitable for your theme, subject and occasion and show off your own personal designer edge!

Objective

How will you create your design practically? Looking at the visuals and 'points of interest' you have decided on; think about what medium you will use to create them. You might want to hand paint an image onto the cake or it may be more suitable to create it out of icing 3 dimensionally, what would be more effective? Would it look better in 3D, boldly taking pride of place or simply repeated 2 dimensionally around the base? Create an 'idea sheet'; draw out the outline of your cake again, but this time bigger and multiple times. Start to sketch out different ideas of where to place things, keeping in mind about what medium would be best to use. When you are happy with one of the sketches and you have decided on the positioning, think in more depth about the medium you will use to create the decorations. What strength of icing will you need for something 3D or free standing? What tools will you need to cut that shape? How long will you need to create that in advance so that you can hand paint it? I always make these sorts of notes on my

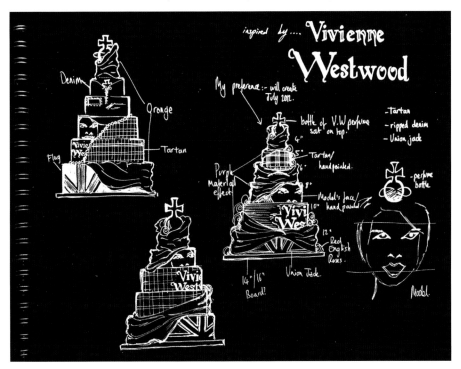

design sheet so I am prepared before I start to begin creating the design physically; it is easier doing it this way round as you will have less to worry about when you do.

Finally, make a list of all the materials you will need, and once you have got them all you are ready to start.

In this section, I have shown 4 examples of different designs created from this process. Throughout the book, you will learn how to use different, signature techniques I have devised. There are also 2, in depth, step-by-step guides, which include many of my signature techniques in action, helping you understand how the whole process works.

Please read the Final Word at the back of the book for a final re-cap before you begin to create a 'Unique' design of your own.

— *Passion Birds* —

With the 'craze' of vintage bird cages hitting weddings everywhere, and having had booked for 2012 a lot of cakes based on this theme, I designed this cake at the end of 2011 so my prospective clients could see and get ideas of how to represent this theme in many different ways.

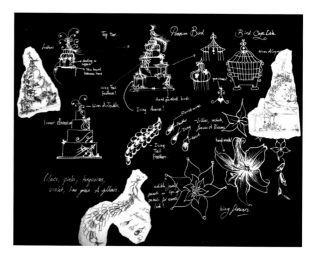

First, when sketching the different types of bird cages, I started to see many different types of swirls and patterns in the wires that they were constructed from. It seemed that the older the cage, the more elaborate the design. Straight away I knew these elements of the design were going to be three dimensional, the bird cages consisted of thin wire bars, and I would have to create these by using the Squires Kitchen florist paste, and then leave to dry before constructing the cage with edible glue. The base of the bird cage bars would sit, cemented within the fondant icing cake for extra support, the fondant would act as a foundation for the bars.

When sketching a bird to sit amongst the cage design, it was obvious that it should appear delicate and enchanted, with colours of beauty and paradise. The bird, I decided, should be the focal point of the top tier decoration, and 'fondant flowers' should be the throne for it to sit on. I began to think about the cake's construction, I would build the bird around a long bamboo skewer that would be pushed into the top and descend through the middle of the tiers, helping them to stay in place.

The second focal point, I thought, should be two passion birds meeting in the middle (as this is a wedding cake design), and there was no better way to display them than to use the hand painted technique. To create the effect of the passion birds being in flight, I decided I would push into the cake some 'tail feathers', adding a three dimensional element to the hand painted birds.

— Oriental Antique —

Last year, I took my children for a visit to the V&A in London and was totally inspired by their display of antique dark oak furniture, with embedded pearls and oriental style metal clasps and corner brackets. The fine attention to detail had me fixated on every single millimetre of the designs.

Once I had returned home, I simply had to search for 'Oriental Antique' furniture and I began to start to sketch the repetitive patterns, floral shapes and metallic colours. I immediately visualised a masculine, black stacked cake (to represent the feel of the dark oak furniture), with focal points of oriental patterning. I wanted to have a 'quilted' tier, embedded with edible pearls, and finally dusted with metallic powders to give the effect of the varnished wood. I would use a new makeup sponge to apply the powder to the icing when dry.

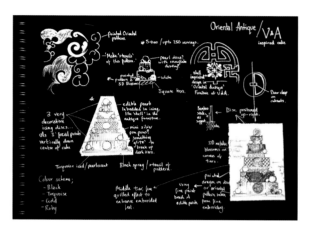

I also decided that I wanted the focal points to stand vertically, off the surface of the cake, so I would prepare the discs from our 'strong' icing. Rolling it out to around 2mm thickness, cutting around a saucer with a craft knife and leaving to dry before hand painting on the repetitive oriental patterns in the colours I found in my research.

The floral patterns and swirls, which I felt gave the strongest representation of the oriental style, would be displayed on the front side of the cake. To give that layered effect, I decided each layer would be made of mixed mediums i.e. iced in one layer of colour, a second layer of pattern (created by edible black spray-on colouring and stencils I cut from paper for a nice neat finish) and a third layer cut out of black fondant icing.

To soften the edges of this masculine design, I wanted to give it a feminine touch by decorating it with oriental style flowers. Here came my invention of the 'star flower', (see 'Fondant Flowers' page 56 onwards), these would finish my design off perfectly!

— Character Cake —

I designed this character cake for my children. Their love for reading story books was my inspiration to create a cake that brought the story to life!

When I began the design sheet, it was important that I included all the aspects of children's story books that had captured their imaginations. The brightly coloured illustrations and fantasy element really kept children and adults alike glued to the story. I decided I would re-create and construct an 'impossible' fantasy cake. Planning out the construction of the cake on the design sheet, made the process of physically making the cake easier to begin.

For me, the hand painted scenes/illustrations from story books were a 'must have' on the base of the cake. This would make the children want to follow the design around the cake, like they would when turning the pages to reach the end of the story.

Carving the hat from the sponge would be the fun bit. I would have to use a carving knife [see 'Carving and Buttercreaming' page 16-17] and by making repeated vertical cuts, the shape of the hat should quickly take form. I would then ice it, and place it on the cake in a position where it would appear to defy gravity. I decided to build the cat around a bamboo skewer, like the bird, but this time from Squires Kitchen florist paste, which would allow the character to stand firm and strong, even with its delicate features.

All children love cupcakes at parties and celebrations, so incorporating the theme/design on to them was completely necessary! I decided I would place them on a 2 tier stand to finish off the design nicely.

Equipment

When starting a business on next to nothing, with 3 children to support, it was essential that I only bought the equipment I needed for cake decorating. There are so many products on the market and it is easy to believe that it's an expensive business to get into, however what do these products do? Most of them do everything for you. I.e. butterfly plungers, stencils for painting etc, but where's the fun, skill or creativity in that?

Straight away, all of these types of products were crossed off my list. I didn't want to produce decorations that looked like everyone else's; straight off the production line. A simple and cheap craft knife will enable you to cut out any decoration shape that you want. You will be the designer, the artist, the creator, developing your own style and originality.

I knew that the preparation of icing was important, so my first investment was a non-stick rolling pin and board. These would guarantee a smooth surface for my icing, and the board would allow me to create smaller decorations, without the worry of them sticking.

The next items I purchased were a 99p set of plastic spatulas and a 'turn table'. These would be essential for smoothing the icing on the cakes. The combination of turning the cake and applying pressure with the spatula is a skill to practice for a perfectly smooth cake. The only other tool you need to assist this process is your hand!

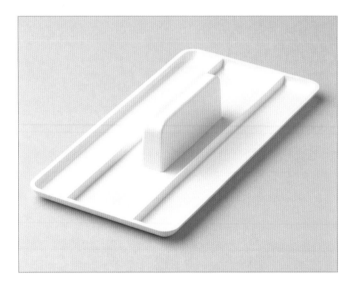

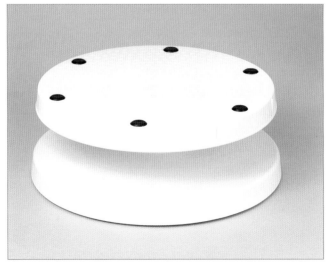

Your hand- the best tool!

Your hands also kneed your icing to an ideal temperature, which then makes decorating your cake so much easier and avoids any cracks or splinters in the icing before smoothing. When colouring icing with your hands, you are also getting the fonadant to the right temperature; killing 2 birds with 1 stone!

It is not just about using your hands as tools but it's about connecting with your materials; think like a sculptor rather than a cake decorator.

1: THE INDEX FINGER AND THUMB
USE THESE TOOLS FOR CREATING FOLDS IN THE 'WRAP' EFFECT.

2: THE DISTAL PHALANX
THE DISTAL PHALANX OF YOUR INDEX FINGER IS PERFECT FOR APPLYING EDIBLE GLUE AND GLITTERS ON TO YOUR ICING DECORATIONS.

3: INDEX AND MIDDLE FINGER
USE THESE TWO TOOLS TO SMOOTH AND SHARPEN THE EDGE AROUND YOUR CAKE BOARDS TO PERFECTION, BEFORE ADDING RIBBON.

4: THE THENAR
THIS TOOL IS PERFECT FOR SMOOTHING OVER ICED CUP-CAKES TO GIVE A PERFECT FINISH.

5: THE HYPOTHENAR
THIS TOOL IS YOUR MOST VALUABLE! IT REMAINS ALMOST CONSTANT TEMP SO DOESN'T GET TO HOT AND STICK TO ICING. IT IS PADDED SO IT IS ABLE TO MOULD ITSELF AROUND ICING, PERFECT FOR SMOOTHING YOUR CAKES AND CAKE BOARDS.

6: THE THENAR AND THE HYPOTHENAR
PUSHING THESE TWO PARTS OF YOUR HAND TOGETHER CREATES A RIGHT ANGLE, WHICH IS PERFECT FOR SMOOTHING AND CREATING A SHARP EDGE AROUND YOUR CAKE.

7: THE SIDE OF YOUR LITTLE FINGER
THIS TOOL IS NARROW ENOUGH TO SMOOTH THE CREASES OF ANY DECORATION, ESPECIALLY ICING STRIPS OR 'CANDY STRIPES'.

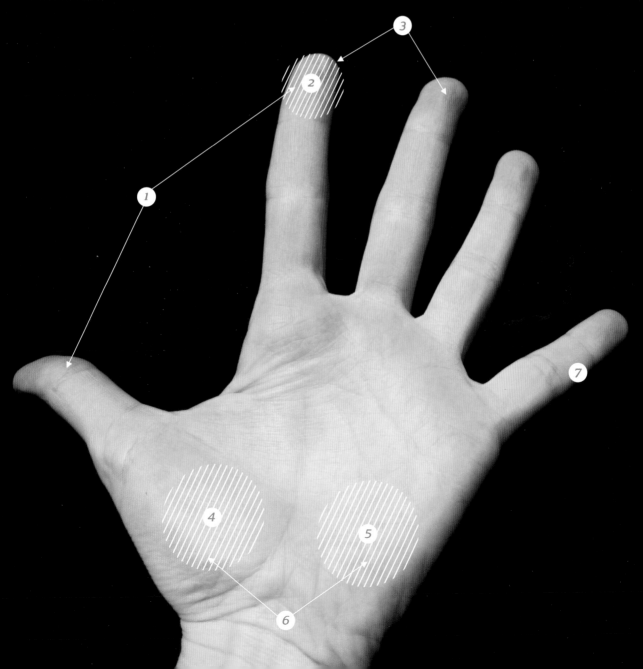

— Carving and Buttercreaming —

First of all, I don't believe in buying novelty shaped cake tins as they are extremely expensive and it is very unlikely you will get your moneys worth; not to mention your cake will end up looking like every other cake created from that mass produced tin. When carving your own cakes from a basic circular or square tin, you are in control of the size, shape, font style (for numbered or lettered cakes), height and overall appearance.

For example, when carving the dress of a princess doll cake, you can decide the style of the skirt, classical and slim or full and voluptuous, something designed instead of from a tin! This also applies to 'Football tins/cakes', carve your own and you will have the freedom to adapt to the style of ball require for your design, e.g. rugby, cricket, American football.

Whatever shaped cake you are carving, always prepare the cake inside first by adding your desired fillings e.g. jam and buttercream. When carving something more difficult, always have an image of your object to follow. Visualise the shape you want to create within the sponge, keep looking at the image and using your hand eye co-ordination, guide your knife through the sponge accordingly, a bread knife, I find, is perfect for carving sponge. Use your knife to record measurements to keep your cake to scale. If you are not confident with your incisions, take off less to begin with as you can always remove more later; it is much harder to add cake on if you cut off too much. Remember you are in control of the knife and this way you have the freedom to create something unique, rather than from a production line cake tin.

The most technical type of cake to carve is probably the 'car cake'. Whether you desire to create a character/cartoon style car or a sporty looking racing car, you need to look closely from every angle and make several small, diagonal, to scale cuts into the sponge.

— Tips for carving car cakes —

1. Start by cutting the width and the length of the cake, followed by the height, so you are beginning with a 'brick' shaped block of sponge.

2. Next, work out which portion of the top of the brick will be the roof of the car. Leave this area and carve each side to create the front and back windscreen. Looking at the pictures of your chosen car, concentrate on the angles of the front and back windows and recreate them with your carving knife.

3. To complete the overall shape of your car, follow the angles of the bonnet and boot with your knife through the sponge.

4. Last of all; follow your pictures to make small, carved incisions to shape the sides, including the doors, wings and wheel arches.

Once your cake is prepared to your desired shape, cover the exterior with some soft buttercream using a plastic spatula. This creates a final smooth surface, enabling your icing to stick to the cake when decorating [see 'Icing your cake' on the following page]. However, please remember, buttercreaming your cake will not allow you to defy the laws of gravity! Fondant icing will not stick to a cake side which is over hanging, due to the weight the icing, it will eventually fall away.

TIP: WHIP YOUR BUTTERCREAM UNTIL IT IS EXTREMELY SOFT, BEFORE APPLYING TO THE EXTERIOR OF YOUR CAKE. THIS WILL ENABLE YOU TO BUTTERCREAM FRESHLY CARVED AREAS WITHOUT PULLING AND RIPPING THE SPONGE.

— Carving 'wonky cakes' —

Wonky cakes are so simple to create and the effect is amazing!

1. With your carving knife, cut diagonally straight through the top layer, then carefully remove it.

2. Place a little jam or buttercream on the freshly cut sponge to act like a glue.

3. Place the diagonally cut sponge that you took off in step 1 back on but turn it 180°, so that the two wide ends and the two narrow ends are meeting each other, trim the sides.

4. Finally buttercream the whole exterior and decorate the cake as normal.

5. If you require another layer, repeat the process the opposite way around with a smaller cake

— *Icing Your Cake* —

Once your cake is prepared to the size and style you require and the exterior is thinly covered in buttercream [see 'Carving and Buttercreaming' on the previous pages], you are ready to ice your cake!

I use 'fondant icing' to cover all of my cakes - this is primarily due to it's similarity to clay; it is smooth and allows you to sculpt it to your own specifications. Also, because it is very easy to colour and decorations can be applied without tarnishing the surface.

I use Renshaws pre-coloured icing in black and red as it would require a lot of food colouring to get the pigmentations that strong when starting with white/ivory. Buying them already coloured saves an awful lot of time and mess!

TIP: ONCE YOU HAVE THE ICING THE COLOUR YOU REQUIRE, KNEED IT UNTIL IT'S AT THE SAME TEMPERATURE AS YOUR HANDS. GENTLY WARMING THE ICING THIS WAY WILL PREVENT CRACKS AND MAKE IT EASIER TO SMOOTH WHEN APPLIED TO THE CAKE, CREATING A SOFTER FINISH.

Lightly sprinkle icing sugar on your work surface, and begin to roll out your icing using a non-stick rolling pin. This way you will not need to turn the icing over, getting icing sugar on your clean icing surface. This is especially important when rolling coloured icing, as you can imagine, white streaks on black icing will ruin your finish.

Once you have rolled out the icing to about 1cm in thickness and checked that it is an even thickness throughout, begin to roll it onto the non-stick rolling pin, lifting it off the surface. As you become more confident at icing your cake, you may reduce the thickness.

DEBORAH'S TIP: WHEN TRYING TO JUDGE WHETHER YOU HAVE

ROLLED OUT A LARGE ENOUGH AREA OF ICING TO COVER YOUR CAKE, PICK UP YOUR CAKE BOARD AND HOLD IT OVER THE ICING. THE ICING SHOULD EXCEED THE SIZE OF THE BOARD AND YOU SHOULD BE ABLE TO JUDGE WHETHER YOU'LL HAVE ENOUGH TO COVER THE SIDES.

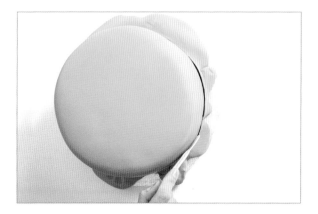

When I first saw Deborah doing this, I thought to myself; what on Earth is she doing? But it really works. Great tip, Deborah!

Immediately transport the icing over to your prepared cake and meet the edge of your icing to the base of the cake. Gently unroll the fondant onto the cake, lowering it onto the surface as you do so.

Gently press the icing against the buttercreamed surface of the cake with your hands, so that it sticks to the sides. Be careful not to crease or overlap the icing. Use a 'smoother' or plastic spatula to firmly press the icing to the top of the cake.

With the edge of a plastic spatula, cut off any excess icing from the base of the cake, roll it into a ball and put it to one side to use later for making icing flowers or decorations on wires etc.

TIP: The best way to store this icing is in an airtight container, food bag or to wrap it up in cling film to prevent it from drying out.

Finally, spend a few minutes going over the cake once more, smoothing and evening out any bumps to give a perfect levelled finish. No tool is better than using your hands for this job.

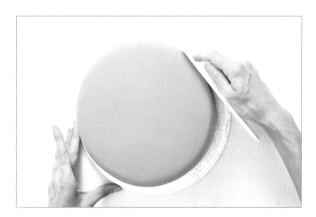

Stacking

Stacking is a lot to do with common sense, knowing the weight of your tiers, what will take extra weight and what will not. For example, a fruitcake stacked on top of a sponge would squash it, but a sponge would sit on top of a fruitcake without needing any support at all.

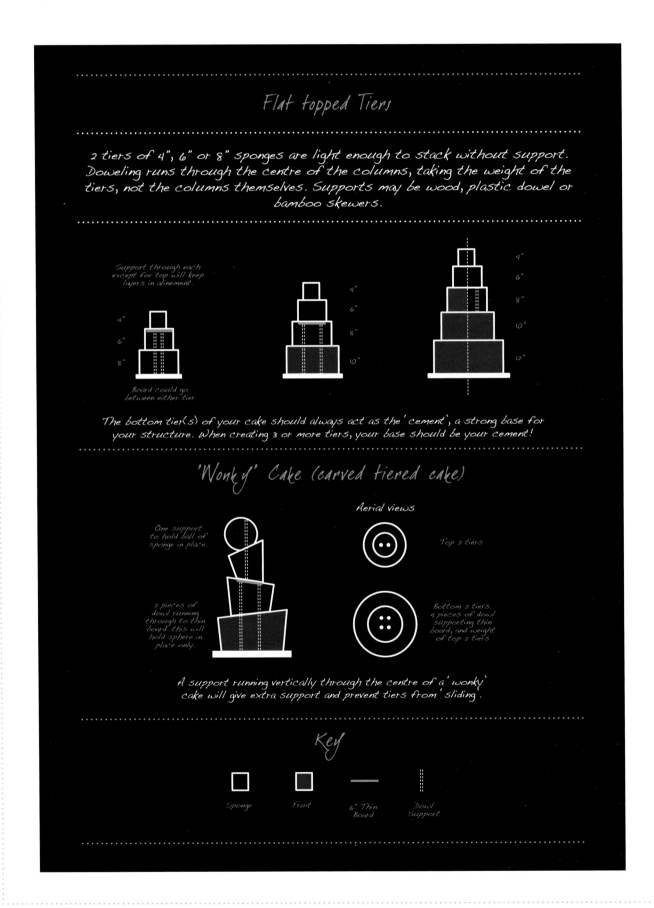

Flat topped Tiers

2 tiers of 4", 6" or 8" sponges are light enough to stack without support. Doweling runs through the centre of the columns, taking the weight of the tiers, not the columns themselves. Supports may be wood, plastic dowel or bamboo skewers.

Support through each except for top will keep layers in alinement.

4"
6"
8"

Board could go between either tier

4"
6"
8"
10"

4"
6"
8"
10"
12"

The bottom tier(s) of your cake should always act as the 'cement', a strong base for your structure. When creating 3 or more tiers, your base should be your cement!

'Wonky' Cake (carved tiered cake)

Aerial views

One support to hold ball of sponge in place.

2 pieces of dowl running through to thin board. this will hold sphere in place only.

Top 2 tiers

Bottom 2 tiers. 4 pieces of dowl supporting thin board, and weight of top 2 tiers

A support running vertically through the centre of a 'wonky' cake will give extra support and prevent tiers from 'sliding'.

Key

Sponge   Fruit   6" Thin Board   Dowl Support

TIP: I PREFER TO USE BAMBOO SKEWERS (SUCH AS YOU WOULD USE FOR KEBABS WHEN COOKING), RATHER THAN WOODEN DOWELING WITH SMALLER CAKES. BAMBOO IS VERY STRONG AND NOT AS WIDE AS DOWELING, MAKING ITS INCISION THROUGH THE CAKE EASIER. IT IS ALSO EASIER TO CUT TO SIZE (EASILY DONE WITH KITCHEN SCISSORS RATHER THAN A SAW) AND WHEN YOU NEED EXTRA SUPPORT IN A SMALL AREA, I.E. THROUGH A FIGURE OR TOWER, IT IS NARROW ENOUGH TO COMPLY. NOT MENTIONING HOW MUCH CHEAPER IT IS TO PURCHASE.

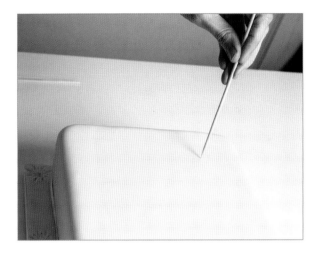

The combination of doweling/bamboo skewers with a thin cake board under the lighter tiers, is safe and secure enough to hold your stacked cake tiers in place. When constructing your already iced cake tiers, just ask yourself, "Where do I need support?" followed by, "Which tiers are solid/strong enough to hold the support?" The rest is simply stacking the cakes in order.

When cutting the supports to size, firstly you need to place them vertically through the centre of the cake and mark them slightly below the surface of the icing. Then remove them gently, cut at the mark and replace them back into the cake.

Some thick Royal icing, made from icing sugar, egg whites and a little lemon juice, makes a good 'cement' to use on the tops of the cut skewers/ doweling. This holds the thin cake boards on top securely in place.

TIP: ANY VISIBLE THIN BOARD ONCE STACKED MAY BE HIDDEN BY A RIBBON AROUND THE BASE OF THE CAKE.

Signature Techniques:

Wrap

Frills

Quilted Effect

Edible Painting

FONDANT FLOWERS

Lettering

Wrap

"I really love your use of the material wrap effect. Your steps to make the 'wrap' were so simple and easy to follow, just need to practice the technique now!"

\- Hannah Campion

Wrap Effect

When I first designed the 'wrap effect', my aim was to create a simple yet dramatic looking cake. With a black biro on a torn piece of note paper, I quickly sketched a design that looked like a cake wrapped in material. Believe it or not I only produced this one rough sketch as I knew straight away that it was exactly what I was looking for! From the black biro on the white note paper the colour scheme revealed itself. I would create a dramatic black cake with white roses.

I showed the design to my staff who said "Wow! But how are you going to create that out of icing?" That was a question I hadn't really given much thought to yet. I prepared and plainly iced all of the cake tiers with black fondant icing. I looked at the remainder of the fondant icing and started to shape it into material like pieces. I thought to myself 'How does material look? What would it look like if it was wrapped around a cake?', whilst visualising then creating the creases and folds.

When it came to attaching the 'material wrap' icing onto the cake, I applied edible glue on to the previously iced surface. When I lifted the pieces of icing and began to wrap them around the cake to attach them, I realised that they took their own form. They seemed to naturally hug the cake and the way the light hit every crease and fold gave an appearance of sheer class!

The 'material wrap effect' has become by far my most popular design and signature piece. Over the last 3 years it has been developed and used for many celebration cakes in all different colours, complimented by various different themes and designs. It definitely is a 'traffic stopper' in my shop window!

★ ★

"Dear Danielle, a huge thank you for our wedding cake, it was absolutely amazing and we had so many comments about it- it matched the bridesmaids' dresses perfectly. We really appreciate all the time and effort you put into it. Thanks again"

- Clare and Declan

★ ★

— *Fondant is **not** just for covering!* —

The word 'fondant' originates from the French word for 'melting' and it is easy to see why this particular recipe of icing was given this name. This soft, dough like icing becomes extremely pliable when kneaded, making it easy to sculpt when decorating your cakes.

Traditionally, cakes were covered with a wet Royal icing or buttercream; however using this it takes more time to create a smooth finish and limits the size and strength of the decorations you can create to go on top. Fondant icing has enabled us to exceed our design expectations, so see it as a sculpting material instead of just a simple cake covering.

Creating a fondant icing covered cake with a smooth finish is a technical skill which we should all practice and try to perfect, but why stop there? You can be taught how to bake and cover a cake, cut out decorations and stick them on, but why limit yourself to just that? Whilst kneading the fondant, you become familiar with it's pliability and it's structure; you will get an idea of what it is capable of producing. Use it to it's full potential, roll it, cut it, bend it, pull it and mould it into your desired shape.

— *Materials* —

Rolled fondant icing can be made from scratch from sugar, water, gelatine (or agar if vegetarian) and glycerine, but I would highly recommend purchasing our own Ivory/white fondant icing. Not only does it have a delicious aroma and light vanilla flavour, but it is extremely malleable and will not crack when moulded into challenging shapes and designs. I like to colour my icing myself but with strong colours, such as black and red, I definitely recommend that you purchase "Renshaws" pre-coloured fondant icing, as it requires a huge amount of food colouring to achieve a good hue.

— *Preparation* —

For the 'wrap' technique, after acquiring your fondant icing all you need is a non-stick rolling pin, a plastic spatula or craft knife, for cutting through the icing and the essential tool for this technique - your hands!

The 'wrap' technique step by step

— Step 1 —

Knead a fist sized ball of black fondant icing with your hands, increasing its temperature until it is soft and pliable. This is important to do before using the icing as it will prevent any cracking or splitting whilst you are sculpting it on the cake.

Roll out the icing into a long oval shape; you can do this by applying more pressure when rolling vertically. Continue rolling until the icing is just a few millimetres in thickness.

TIP: WHEN ROLLING OUT THE BLACK ICING, YOU MAY LIGHTLY COVER THE SURFACE WITH ICING SUGAR, TO ENSURE IT DOESN'T STICK TO THE SURFACE, BUT DO NOT TURN THE ICING OVER AS THE ICING SUGAR WILL MARK THE BLACK. STICKING IS AVOIDED BY USING A NON-STICK ROLLING PIN ANYWAY.

— Step 2 —

Take your plastic spatula in your stronger hand and gently hold the rolled out icing with your other to prevent any movement. Cut through the icing with the spatula, pulling away from your resting hand to create a long, arched curve, ending at the opposite end of the oval to where you started.

Make sure your spatula is held firmly, push down hard with it into the surface and move it slowly. This will ensure the icing is cut cleanly and with control, without any wobbles or tears.

— Step 3 —

Repeat the same procedure, creating a symmetrical arch on the bottom side of the oval. Use your resting hand to hold the icing still as you cut along.

Move away all of the cut off pieces and roll them into a ball to prevent the icing from drying out quickly; you can use this icing again for your next piece of 'wrap'.

You should now be faced with a piece of flat rolled out icing, resembling an oval with pointed ends, a sort of leaf shape. Now it's time to make it look like a piece of material.

— Step 4 —

Carefully tuck the edge of the icing, which is furthest away from you, under itself, to create a rim along the top. Gently smooth the rim by keeping it in between your middle and index fingers and moving your hand horizontally, from left to right, repeatedly, until there is a little shine to its surface. This is the first fold of your material.

— Step 5 —

Lift one end of the icing with your stronger hand and place the middle of your other hand underneath, to create a fold in the centre of the icing. Using your index and middle fingers of your stronger hand, once again pinch the fold created by your other hand, to prevent it from flattening against the surface. This is the beginning of your centre fold in the material.

— Step 6 —

Continue pinching the icing along the centre of the icing 'wrap', moving away from the side you started at, but stopping in the middle, producing a centre fold. Again, smooth the icing until you create a soft shine.

— Step 7 —

Once you've reached the middle of the 'wrap', move to the opposite end of the icing and repeat steps 5 and 6.

Working from each end of the wrap, instead of working all the way through from one end to the other, will prevent knuckle marks and the icing tearing by it being lifted too high.

— Step 8 —

Finally, to finish off your 'wrap', lift the remaining flat edge of the icing which is closest to you and repeat step 4, tucking it underneath itself and then smoothing the rim between your fingers.

Spending a couple of minutes smoothing each of the folds/rims will make the icing look like a piece of material; it's this preparation that will complete the illusion. [See Thank You Cake for The Royal Ballet page 82]

There are no set sizing techniques I use when covering each tier as I believe that its unique appearance is down to the random application of each 'wrap' icing. Each 'wrap' is individual and when applying them it becomes obvious where they will lay and fold onto the surface of the cake. Your hands have sculpted each 'wrap', you know the pliability of the icing, so simply guide each piece onto the already iced and glued surface of the cake, directing it as if it was 'material' embracing the cake.

This technique may be used to fully or partly decorate a cake, depending on your design.

★ ★

"We would like to say a massive 'thank-you' for making us the most wonderful cake for our wedding. The whole ensemble looked stunning and we will certainly recommend you to others planning a celebration. You <u>truly</u> are a small company who produces <u>big things!</u> Thank you once again."
- Julie and Clive

★ ★

Frills

My inspiration to create the 'frill' design came from English frilly lace and netting, like the netting on a tutu or an underskirt; quaint and pretty. To replicate the effect and work out how to create it with icing, I first had to think about how it is created using net material. Quite simply the effect is based on using multiple, thin horizontal layers of netting with frilled edges.

Then I asked myself, "What material would be best to use?" Each frill would have to be very thinly rolled out at the edges and hold itself in a horizontal position without breaking, so I decided a strong icing (sugar paste) was required. I would have to make a lot of frills, so there would be plenty of layers close together to give the fuller frilled effect I wanted. I decided it would be best to create each frill, one by one; this takes a lot of time but is definitely worth it.

The first frilled cake I made was a three tier ivory design, finished with a simple ribbon between the tiers to create a 'pompom' type look. I gently eased each 'frill' into position on the sides of the already iced (with fondant icing) cake, and then fixed them in place with edible glue. That was all it took, surprisingly.

The second frill design was a pink cake that I designed for a bridal magazine for their feature, 'the best of the best'. This time I coloured the frills deep pink at the bottom and as the frills got higher, their shade of pink got lighter, so that the top of the tier was baby pink. I used this gradual gradient of colour to add another dimension to the design, it gave the frills more depth and a fuller appearance overall. The tips of the icing frills against the black background, gave the cake a truly dramatic feel.

When I designed my Alexander McQueen inspired cake, I researched his signature dresses and surface patterns, which mainly consisted of bold prints. Repeatedly, I saw dresses with frilly underskirts and snagged material on top. I drew out a few designs, deciding to use peacock style feathers as my bold print and theme. My final design consisted of, a bird silhouette, real peacock feathers as well as the print hand painted onto icing, cream frills representing the underskirts, with a blue draped material wrap effect as the snagged material skirt.

— Materials —

When deciding on which strengths of icing you need for your cake designs, don't always look to the obvious. For example, when I came across traditional flower pastes, I discovered they were for creating large, delicate, thin petals that would hold without any internal support, ideal for an icing frill. The materials you use are essential to the success of your designed decorations, so find out what the product's capability is, rather than what it is traditionally used for, and experiment. I did and the outcome was that the 'strong' icing was perfect for creating the finer decorations.

— Finishes On Your Decorations —

The 'frilled effect' may be finished off with some edible lustre or the edges could even be tinted with some edible paint, like the edges of a carnation petal.

Frills Step by Step

— Prep. —

Pinch a small ball (about the size of a broad bean) of strong icing from the foil pouch and quickly reseal after. Knead the paste with your thumbs and fingers, using a fast 'pull and fold' motion, until it is soft and pliable.

— Step 1 —

Place the paste on a non-stick board, and then using a small non-stick rolling pin, begin to roll it out. Start rolling a couple of millimetres from its base, away from you, until the furthest edge from you is paper thin. Keep the edge of the paste closest to you thick; this will enable your 'frill' to stand while drying. This is why you begin rolling 2mm in; you need your 'frill' to have a good structure and strength.

— Step 2 —

Lift the 'frill' gently and run your thumb along the thick base, creating a flat edge. This will be your frill's platform for standing and it will also give it extra strength when you insert it into the fondant iced cake.

Your frill at this stage should be a shell like shape; thick at the base with the paste rolled outwards in all directions, (left, central and right).

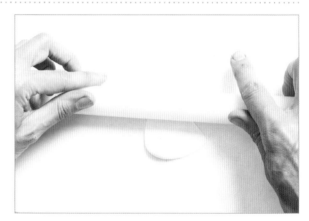

— Step 3 —

Now use a flower tool or the pointed end of a bamboo skewer to press firmly along the thin edge of the paste, rolling it backwards and forwards to create a frilled effect. Don't worry about pressing too firmly as small tears along the edge will just add to the effect, and not ruin it.

— Step 4 —

Lift the frill off the surface of the non-stick board and gently with your index fingers and thumbs, mould horizontal curves on each side. The more depth to the curve the better, but try and make the curves symmetrical, this will add to the full frilled effect when multiple frills are put together.

— *Step 5* —

Now stand the frill on the slightly flattened, thicker edge to dry. This usually takes around 12 hours for maximum strength.

Repeat the process until you have as many frills as needed, this is a timely procedure but the effect it creates 'wows' and bewilders people more than any other decoration I have created.

Standing the frills together while drying will help you work out how many you will need for your design and decoration.

If you have planned to dust, paint or glitter your frills as part of your design, then do it at this stage, once dried but before insertion [see previous page for ideas].

Placing your 'frills' into your decorated cake

When placing the frills into your design, visualise how you would like the overall appearance of the cake to look. With this visualisation in mind, start to build up the frills, every now and then stepping back to take a look, checking it appears as you desire. There is no need for templates, just use your eyes and imagination, along with your design for guidance.

— Step 1 —

Apply some edible glue along the thick end of each frill.

— Step 2 —

Holding the sides of each dried frill, one at a time, gently push them a few millimetres into the fondant icing on the side of the cake.

— Step 3 —

Hold for several seconds so that the frill is at a 90° angle to the cake, then release to see it held unsupported.

— Step 4 —

Repeat the process running left to right along the cakes surface, positioning them so that the curves are as parallel as possible. This will enhance the overall effect.

— Step 5 —

Create multiple rows of frills, so each is staggered similar to a brick laying pattern, until the iced area of your cake is covered.

Your frills will be of different shapes and sizes as this isn't a measured technique, so place the smaller ones towards the base and top edge of the cake, and the larger, more prominent ones in the centre to give that full, puffed out, frilly effect.

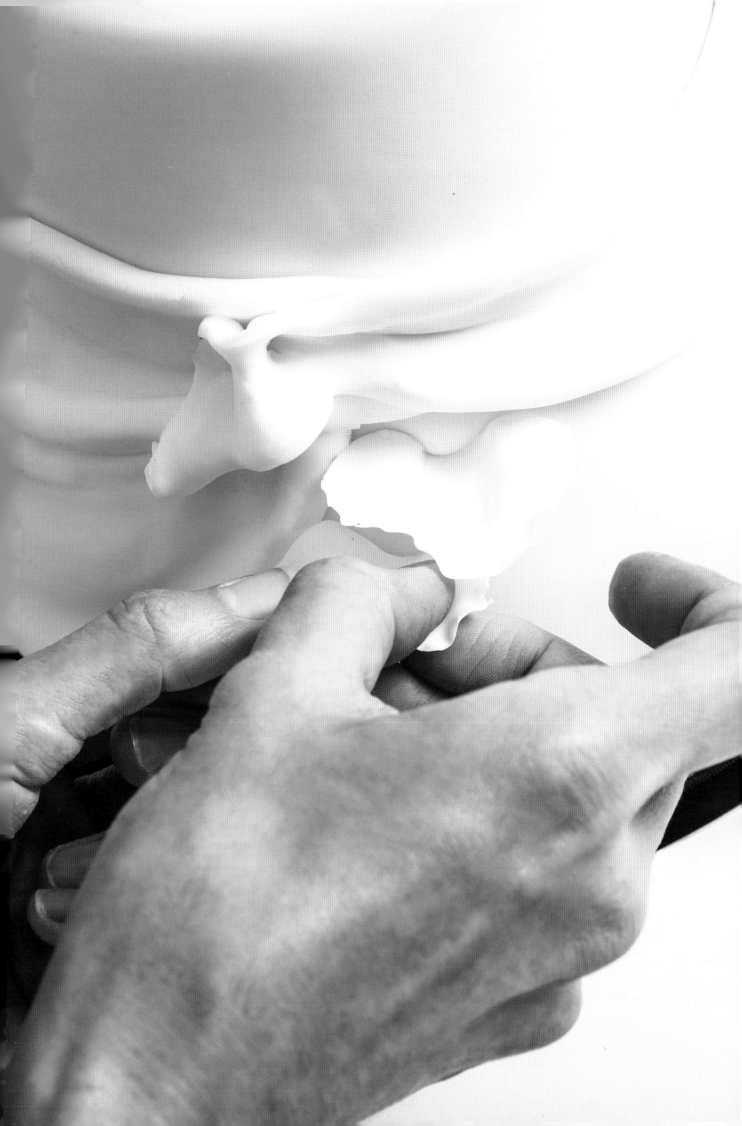

Quilted Effect

★ ★

"STUNNING! Nothing like this when I got married. I'd do it all over again just for this cake!"
- Colette Hickling

★ ★

— Quilting Foreword —

The quilting technique is one of the most simple, yet most effective, of all the cake techniques. The majority of people who walk into my shop will head towards the single tier, ivory, quilted cake I have on display and immediately begin to imagine how they could adapt their theme to include the technique.

The technique where material is pinned to create this padded appearance is traditionally called 'Tufting', but my clients have called this the Quilted Effect when ordering their cakes for so long now, it's stuck!

My friend and work colleague, Deborah, was the one who first sketched this design for me to create and, having never attempted anything like it before, I had to switch my 'logical' head on! To create a padded illusion effect, I would have to make incisions into the icing, giving an appearance of depth and texture.

Using a plastic spatula, I made repeated, diagonal incisions, parallel to one another and equally spaced apart around the sides of each tier. First left to right, then right to left, the diamond shapes I created appeared to give the quilted effect on the surface of the icing. Then it was time to add some detail to bring the quilting to life.

When looking at something like a 'Chesterfield' armchair, you see its tight surface, pinned down with studs, and a shiny appearance where the covering is holding the stuffing. Because of this, I felt it important to give that shine on the surface of the icing, also to give it an added 3D impression. I did this by dabbing a little "snowflake" edible dusting powder, with a small dry sponge, in the centre of each diamond.

Quilting diamonds can be made as small or as large as you like, depending on the effect you are aiming for.

Here I've produced small diamond shapes to create a finer quilted effect. I inserted small edible pearls into the corner of each diamond to recreate the appearance of antique carved oak furniture, with mother of pearl inserts. Once the icing had dried to form a firm exterior, I dusted the centre of each diamond with some edible gold dusting powder for extra effect.

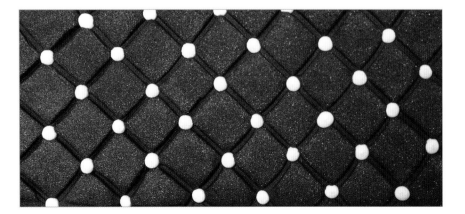

In the 'Oriental Antique' design [See 'Design Guide'], I added the quilted effect to the centre tier to 'soften' the overall appearance and give another dimension to the finished piece.

TOOLS: *THE PLASTIC SPATULA IS DEFINITELY YOUR BEST FRIEND WHEN CREATING THE QUILTED TECHNIQUE!*

— Finish On the Cake Surface —

When creating the quilted technique, I want to give the impression of fabric, so the finish on the cake is very important i.e. matte icing wouldn't create the shine given by a stretched material which is being pinned by studs and padded to its fullest capacity.

There are two materials that I use that will create such an effect, one is an edible glaze [as featured on page 59] and the other is an edible lustre from "Sugarflair" called "Snowflake" - this is my preferred choice. The 'snowflake' patina is a fine, white and shimmery dust powder. Once you have completed the quilted technique on your cake, the lustre may be applied in one of two ways; the first is by

diffuser and the second is using a sponge in a gentle dabbing motion. I use a clean makeup sponge to apply the sheen to give an even coat all over the surface of the iced cake. I find the lustre gives a 'satin' type finish which gives a touch of elegance to the quilted effect. The glaze creates a harder shine, giving a 'plastic' type finish. Choose your finish depending on what style of cake you are going for.

— Preparing Your Cake for 'Quilting' —

Once your cake is smoothly iced with fondant icing [see 'Icing Your Cake' page 24-25], to prepare for 'quilting' there is one more extra step to take. With a plastic spatula, go around the base of the cake at a 45° angle. This gives the effect that the icing is 'tucked in', like the edge of a cushion. Once you have completed this step, you are ready to start quilting.

Step by Step: Creating the quilted effect

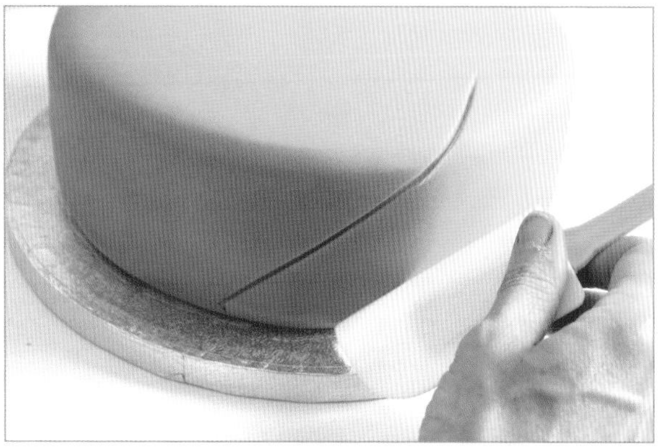

— Step 1 —

Take your fondant iced cake and begin by holding your plastic spatula diagonally at 'one o'clock.' Line the spatula up to the side of the cake before pressing the tip towards the base, applying a small amount of pressure. Each incision should only be a couple of millimetres deep.

— Step 2 —

Drag the spatula gently into the icing, up and over the side of the cake, creating a diagonal line until you reach about an inch over the top. The reason you are stopping here is because if you carry on, the lines will end up crossing unevenly in the centre. If you are stacking tiers that are decorated using this technique, the lines will appear as if they are continued as there is usually about an inch difference between tiers.

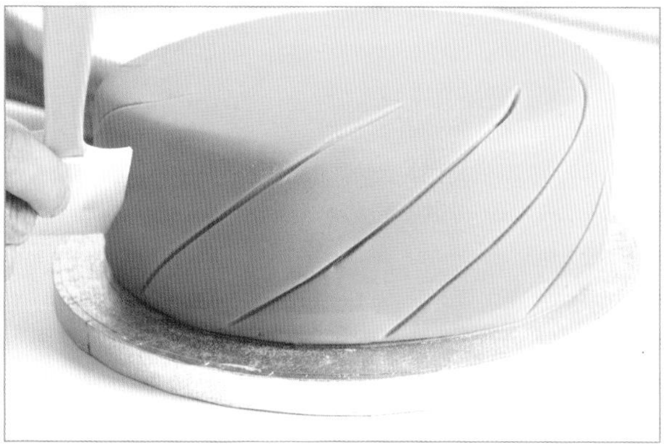

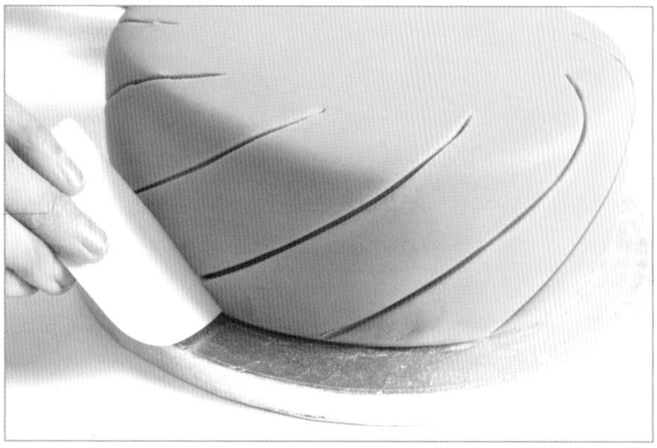

— Step 3 —

Repeat this process around the cake, beginning each line at the base, about 1.5 inches apart. Take your time as you want the lines to be parallel. If you don't feel confident judging the space with your eyes, measure around the base of the cake and make very small marks which will be covered when you use your spatula to create the line. However, I strongly advise you not to do this as I believe using your eyes to judge will help build your confidence in cake decorating.

— Step 4 —

After completing the process one way, begin the other. I start my first line in the opposite direction by creating a small cross with an existing line at the base, making sure that the beginning of each new line is roughly around 1 cm to the right of the existing line.

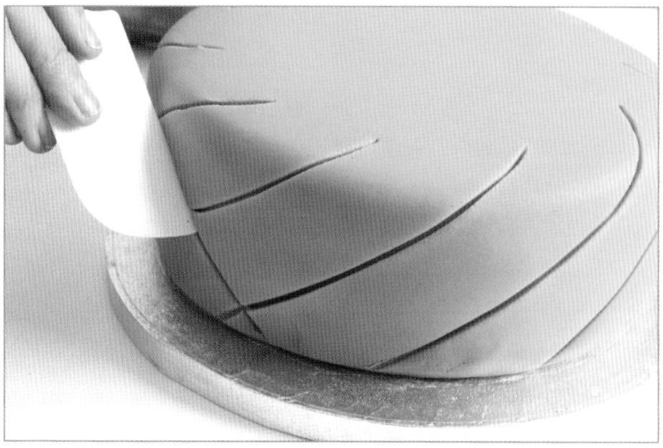

way round until each line is cross[...]
diamond, quilted pattern.

Step 6 —

[...] all the lines are completed, gently go over
[...] again with your spatula, but this time instead
[...] lying pressure, just move your tool from side
[...] e in a slight 'rocking' motion, this will give
[...] iamond a gentle 'padded' effect.

— Step 7 —

Depending on your design and colour [...]
small edible balls in each 'cross' of the [...]
to represent the studs which keep pac[...]
Because the icing is still soft and mo[...]
balls should sit firmly in place withou[...]
using any edible glue.

[...]re you have it, one quilt effect cake

Edible Painting

★ ★ ★ ★ ★ ★ ★ ★ ★ ★ ★ ★ ★ ★ ★ ★ ★ ★ ★

"Danielle, this is beautiful and I love the way you've incorporated the tea-cups!"
-Benessamy Events

★ ★ ★ ★ ★ ★ ★ ★ ★ ★ ★ ★ ★ ★ ★ ★ ★ ★ ★

— *Foreword* —

The reason I created my Edible Painting technique was because I didn't believe in using printed images on cakes. Where is the creativity in that? It would be like saying to an artist, "Why do paintings when you can just take a picture?" Also, with Edible Painting, you are in complete control of where the images are going, e.g. how far a vine will climb up an icing turret or what colour the flowers are on the side of a wedding cake, (which is essential when colour matching with the bridesmaid's dresses). I also like to paint inscriptions on my celebration cakes, instead of doing traditional piped messages, this way I have more control of the thickness of the lettering and style of the font. Plus it's much easier when writing an inscription on the side of a cake!

On my 'English Tea' cake design I wanted to paint an array of flowers which typically grow in any English garden, so roses were an absolute must! I looked at some old china tea-cups I had in the shop and admired the painted flowers which decorated the surface. I replicated this on the tiers of the cake in blues, beige, burgundy and pinks... English Tea!

Being brought up by my grandmother, I was always surrounded by antiques and decorative ornaments. One item that sticks in my mind was a bowl of porcelain roses that were positioned on a table on the landing. They were all shiny and painted in pale pastel colours, so delicate and small I used to fear that when I touched them, they would break. I made the fondant roses to look as traditional as possible, in memory of these porcelain ornaments. I sprayed them with lots of Edible Glaze to make them shine. I mainly use the Glaze on the edible painting once finished to prevent any powdery smudges. I got this idea when I thought about how we would use hairspray on our chalk drawings at Art College to set them so they wouldn't smudge.

"The cake was amazing and had more photos taken than us!!"
-John Wright

— Icing Is Your Canvas —

Once you have perfected your smooth finish to your fondant iced cake, you have a canvas to begin your painting. For you to be able to paint confidently, you need to imagine that the cake is not a cake, but a blank surface for you to produce your art on, like a page in a sketch book. Seeing it any differently will make you nervous, and afraid of ruining the cake. Ironically, it is this fear that will cause you to make mistakes! Relax, take your time and be confident. This is the most important preparation before beginning your edible painting.

— Preparing Your Paint —

My first tip would be to purchase a white plastic palette from an art materials store; they usually only cost a couple of pounds and are very easy to clean. Next, it is very important to have a good quality brush when doing any type of painting, but it is especially important when using edible paints, as the consistency changes and as you are painting on icing, it's hard to adjust any mistakes.

A good quality brush will not only make your painting task easier, but will last longer, without the bristles fraying and sticking out to the sides or even falling out. So spend a couple of pounds extra and invest in a decent brush with high quality soft bristles – this will enable your strokes to glide gently over the surface of the icing, without leaving any scratches or dints. A size '0' or '00' will be the most useful.

To create the edible paint, I use 'sugarflair' edible powders mixed with a dipping solution. Because it is made from a dry powder, the paint becomes gradually thicker as time passes, and after around 24hrs, it will revert back to a powder again. The positive side of this is that as it dries the colour gets stronger, which is particularly useful for creating darker tones and shading. However, the negative side is that you have to keep adding 'dipping solution' and work quickly before it dries out, as thickening paint can effect the quality of your brush strokes in mid flow. But overall, you are in charge of the quality of your materials. My methods are all about having direct contact and control with the materials you are using. You are the artist and the only difference between this and how an artist paints is that it is edible.

Once you have completed your painting, use an edible fixing glaze to prevent any smudging.

CULPITT DIPPING SOLUTION description: 'USE TO COLOUR FLOWERS MADE OUT OF SUGAR OR COLD PORCELAIN OR TO GLAZE LEAVES. ADD LIQUID, PASTE OR POWDER COLOUR TO THE SOLUTION TO DIP FLOWERS. ADD TO CONFECTIONS GLAZE FOR CREATING GLOSSY LEAVES.'

THE EDIBLE GLAZE SPRAY COMES IN SPRAY CAN WHICH CAN BE USED ON CAKES AND CHOCOLATE.

Step by Step: Edible Painting

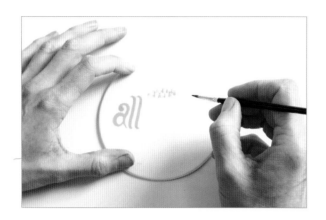

— Step 1 —

When preparing your paint, add a single drop of 'dipping solution' at a time whilst stirring with your brush until you have the right consistency.

TIP: STIR WITH THE SIDE OF YOUR BRUSH TO AVOID DAMAGING THE BRISTLES.

I would advise to create a thin consistency at the start as the paint solution will gradually thicken. Also a thinner, translucent paint is ideal when planning out the design on your cake or icing decoration because it is easy to cover over with a thicker colour.

— Step 2 —

As with any type of painting, always start with the part of design which is furthest away, like the background colour or the object at the back. Divide the painting up into 'layers', the first layer being the one which is furthest away and the last being the one at the front, the one closest to you. When painting an object, the layers are like shading; the layer furthest away from you is darkest and the layer closest is the lightest [see 'Edible Painting' on pages 130 and 131 in the Cupcake Course]. It is good to visualise and have an idea of your layers when mixing your paint palette.

— Step 3 —

Dip the tip of your paint brush into your already-mixed edible paint, and wipe the brush on the side of the palette to prevent any excess paint from spoiling the precision you require.

— Step 4 —

When painting thin lines for small details or inscriptions, ensure that just the tip of the brush has light contact with the icing. Try not to be heavy handed. If you require a bolder line or to fill in a larger area, apply more pressure so that the whole of the brush has contact with the icing. Always continue to move the brush, as keeping it in one spot, especially if the icing is still soft, will cause indentation.

— Step 5 —

For an even colour and no signs of brush strokes, apply a second coat of paint. This may be applied immediately after the first layer, as the paint dries really quickly. Unlike normal paint, the more coats you apply, the stronger the colour will appear. Again, it is up to you to control the quality of the outcome of your painting.

— Step 6 —

Be careful not to touch the surface of your painting, as it will smudge, unless it had been sprayed by the Edible Glaze already. I use my other hand to balance and support the hand holding the brush. However, remember, unlike when leaning your hand on paper or canvas, leaning it on icing will create an indentation, so be careful not to.

— Step 7 —

Finally, cover your painting with an edible glaze. I use a spray on glaze, as a brush on one may spoil the dried powdered painting. Hold the glaze several inches away from the painted surface and spray a small amount lightly over your design. Too much glaze will cause the paint to run or spread. You may use 2 or 3 light sprays of glaze, once each layer is dry, to build up the protection on your painting. You can touch up or paint on top of the glaze if you need to but remember to re-glaze when finished.

When hand painting a design, remember all of these tips, but overall just be confident! Your brush strokes will be better if you do them with confidence and conviction.

★ ★

"Dear Danielle, thank you for creating such a beautiful cake and focal point for our wedding day, we had many compliments on the aesthetics and taste of the cake. Best wishes to you."
-Francis and Katie

★ ★

— *Flower Technique* —

Roses

Roses are the most popular decoration you will ever have to make and this is why a quick and easy method for creating them from icing is an essential for every cake decorator. The traditional way of creating a rose is time consuming, making each petal from sugar craft paste and hanging them from a budded wire; it does create beautiful, large, realistic roses which inevitably sometimes we have to use, but for the majority of your wedding and celebration cakes, a fondant icing rose is much quicker to make and is just as effective!

The great thing about fondant icing is that you can just roll it up into a ball and start again whilst you are practising how to make something! Sugar craft paste, however, dries very quickly and soon becomes brittle and hard, making it very difficult to use repeatedly. Another benefit is that, unlike with sugar craft paste, you don't need to use tools such as non-stick boards, rolling pins and drying racks. To create fondant roses using my flower techniques, you simply need some cellophane that's big enough to fold, an A4 plastic wallet for example, or a cellophane bag would be perfect. This is your non-stick surface! Using items you find around the house instantly saves you money on what would have been expensive equipment. This cellophane can also be used as a non stick surface for moulding other decorations too, such as cars, figures, frills, blossoms and lettering.

Star Flowers

The 'Star Flower' is my own invention; my more contemporary designs required an alternative to the classical rose, something a little less traditional in appearance, something with a more enchanted, bohemian feel and I think this flower fits the brief perfectly!

The most popular colours for these flowers, requested by my clients, are lilac and turquoise, giving the appearance of a complete fantasy flower for any enchanted cake design.

— 5 Rules of Fondant Flowers —

Pressing

When pressing the petals flat between the cellophane, keep the edge of the petal closest to you thick and the edge furthest away from you thin, do not press down in the middle, as you need your petals to be stable.

Holding

You should always hold your petals and flowers by the base at the bottom. Holding them in the middle or at the top will not allow the flower to open naturally.

Applying

With roses, make sure the top of each petal applied is at the same height as the top of the centre petal. Slightly too low, and your rose will progress into spiral shape.

Wrapping

When attaching each petal, always give them a 'little pull' as you are wrapping them around; this will prevent drooping, and will keep the petals upright.

Fixing

When fixing your fondant flower to your cake or cupcake, gently hold it in place by it's centre; this way, you'll have less chance of breaking a petal as the centre is the strongest part of the flower.

"My favourite cake. The roses look so realistic, your great tip about using around the house items such as a plastic wallet made it so simple to create for such a professional finish."
-Hannah Campion

— Creating Fondant Star Flowers —

— Step 1 —

As with the fondant rose, you will be using some folded cellophane as a non-stick surface to press out your petals, so begin by creating balls of icing for each petal required.

With the star flower you will need oval balls of icing, instead of the tear drop shapes needed for the roses, and they will need to be of 3 different sizes:

1 x small oval ball (for the flower centre)
3 x medium oval balls (for the first layer of petals)
5 x large oval balls (for the outer layer of petals)

— Step 2 —

Using the same pressing technique as with the roses, fold over the cellophane and smooth out each petal thinly towards the edge furthest away from you with your index finger, keeping the edge closest to you thick. This is so your petals are stable when you pick them up, and mould easily into a flower, you don't want floppy petals!

— Step 3 —

Once each petal has been pressed out smoothly, peel away the cellophane and lift the smallest petal off the surface. As with the rose, roll this petal using your index finger and thumb at the base, to ensure you don't damage the spiral effect.

— Step 4 —

Next, attach the 3 medium petals. These need to be placed at equal distances around the spiralled centre. Holding the first of the 3 petals with your index finger and thumb at its base and the spiralled centre in the other hand, place them together and gently pull the petal and wrap it around the centre, making sure it stays vertical.

Gently pinch the tip of the petal to create a point.

Repeat this process with the 2 remaining medium petals, so each is placed a third of the way around the centre.

— Step 5 —

Attach the last layer of 5 large petals in exactly the same way, but as they are larger, they will dominate your first layer of 3, so be careful holding the base of your flower between you index finger and thumb.

Visualise a 5 pointed star as you are attaching each petal, making sure that each is positioned a fifth of the way around the base.

Finally, pinch the tip of each petal, drawing it to a point, creating the finishing touch to your fondant star flower!

TIP: TRY AND ATTACH YOUR STAR FLOWERS TO YOUR CAKE STRAIGHT AFTER YOU HAVE MADE THEM AS THE PETALS ARE LONG AND THEY SOMETIMES LOOK NICER IF THEY ARE DRAPED OVER THE CAKE TIERS. ALSO, THERE WILL BE LESS CHANCE OF THE PETAL BREAKING ON APPLICATION...REMEMBER THESE ARE ONLY MADE OF FONDANT ICING, AND BECAUSE THE PETALS ARE LONGER THAN THOSE USED FOR THE ROSE, THEY HAVE A GREATER CHANCE OF SNAPPING ONCE DRY.

Once you have made your fondant flowers by following the step by step instructions, you can add decoration if you wish by dabbing the edges with edible glitter or hand painting them for a more defined look.

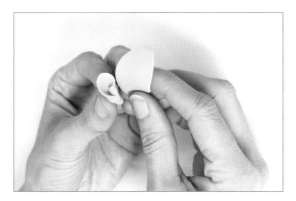

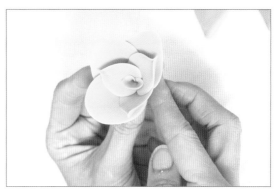
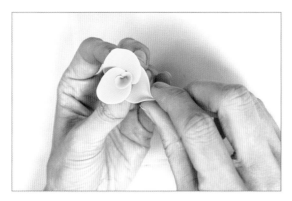

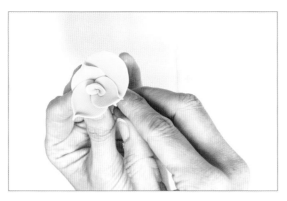

"Dear Danielle, thank you so much
for doing our fantastic wedding
cake. The cake surpassed all of my
expectations and as you can see,
looked fantastic with the wedding
bouquets, the flowers and colours
complimenting each other perfectly."
-Shona and Trevor

— *Lettering* —

When designing a cake around a certain theme, lettering is great to use as a focal point. It also gives the cake a unique twist, as it is different from conventional icing inscriptions. Lettering within your cake design projects a bold message to the viewer and 3D funky fonts can give it that element of fun.

The type of font you use for your lettering will, of course, depend on your theme. Once you have decided on a font you can then decide what technique you will use to create it. There are many different ways you can create lettering; cut it out from my very own 'Medium' icing, hand paint it with edible paints, pipe it on (the traditional way), elevate it on wires or stencil it into the icing of the cake. A good example of this is my cake design 'To Love and Be Loved'.

The theme of this cake was 'Valentines Day', so I started to write down everything that represented Valentines Day to me; red, roses, hearts, cupid and most importantly, messages of love. I searched the top ten love quotes of all time, and the one that came up at number one repeatedly was "To Love and Be Loved." I decided for this to become my lettering. Then I thought about how to present it. I wanted each word to be created differently in the theme of 'love', but first I had to decide on the fonts I would use. I researched the word 'love' and roughly filled an A4 sheet of paper with different ways to write my lettering. I then circled the fonts which I felt represented 'love' the most and recreated them. Eventually I dwindled it down to just five different fonts for five individual words.

Whilst planning out the overall design and deciding which decorations I wanted and where, I plotted how the words would descend down the front of my cake. The position of each word was chosen to draw the viewer's eye to points of interest within the design.

Starting at the top, I decided I would paint the word 'to' on the classic 'heart and arrow' decoration. This was to be painted in black onto the white icing background to give the appearance of a hand written script on a piece of paper, attached to the shooting arrow. The next word, 'Love'; again I wanted

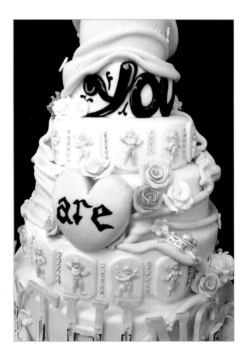

this to be hand painted, but this time on the most iconic 'Valentines Day' symbol, a red heart. The font itself was designed in the shape of a heart to nicely fit inside. The heart needed to be fixed lightly on the front of the cake; it needed to be thin but strong so I decided that it would be best to make it from sugar craft paste. The next word and font, I decided, would simply made out of a long snake shape of white fondant icing covered in glitter and then left to dry before fixing it against a cluster of red roses. The final word, 'loved' was to be placed along the bottom in a way that says it's carefree and on cloud nine. These thicker letters are made up of 50% sugar craft icing and 50% fondant icing, the decoration is then painted on using the hand painting technique once dry, they are finally decorated with pink edible pearls. I've used edible gold paint and pearls within the decoration of the lettering to represent jewellery, the gift, this is the final symbol of 'Valentines Day'.

So there are a few ideas for you to think about while planning lettering within your cake design!

Edible lettering may be created in many different styles and sizes, depending on your theme and overall style and design of the cake. Don't feel that each letter of a word has to be the same font/style, be creative! Think about which method you would like to use to produce your letter and why.

— Hand Painted Fonts —

My favourite method of decorating my letters, is hand painting, as it is limitless, allowing you to use your imagination. When deciding on what to paint on to your fonts, keep in mind your theme as you want everything

to tie in down to the smallest detail. The same applies when deciding on the colours of your edible paints i.e. this picture displaying the word 'LOVED', has been painted with pink hearts to compliment the theme and the edges have been decorated with some pink edible pearls to represent the style of the design and highlight part of the painting.

Another option you could try is to paint a picture onto the letters, to reflect and personalize the word it is spelling. Use your imagination and go beyond the simple steps of just cutting your letters out.

— Decorated Font —

Keeping with your theme, decorate your letters with something that physically connects with your theme (e.g. cake toppings on the word 'CAKE') or something that highlights the style of your design, like glitter on a 'glam' designed cake font.

When applying decoration to your letters, firstly you will need to apply a thin layer of edible glue to the relevant area of the icing font. Once decorated, each letter will need to lie horizontally flat for at least 6 hours, to set before you lift it up and position it on your decorated cake.

A simple shower of edible glitter on a dried icing letter may be fixed with some glaze; the letter may be then lifted and positioned on your cake within a few minutes.

— Candy Twist Fonts —

If you have used a couple of colours to ice your cake, you may be left with a couple of 'cut off bits' which are extremely useful for creating candy twist fonts! Not only does this guarantee that your font colour will co-ordinate with your cake, but it adds an extra dimension to your decoration.

The candy twist technique is simply created by producing long 'sausages' of fondant icing from 2 different colours, placing them next to each other, and rolling them together along your work surface. To give a clean finish, cut the ends off with a craft knife. Then all you need to do is mould it into shape to form your desired letter, leave it overnight to fully dry and attach it directly to your decorated cake.

TIP: FOR LARGER FONTS USE OUR MEDIUM ICING AND IF YOUR LETTERS ARE TO APPEAR THIN AND FREESTANDING USE OUR STRONG ICING PASTE.

Step by Step: Lettering

— Step 1 —

The desired thickness for your lettering determines which icing you need to use. For a thin, dainty font you will need to use my strong icing and for a chunky, dense font, you can use my medium strength icing. Colour your icing to the desired tone with food colouring paste, as you don't want to weaken the structure of the icing by using a liquid colouring.

— Step 2 —

Use a non-stick rolling pin and on a non-stick surface, like a non-stick board or plastic cellophane, to roll your icing to the desired thickness. Using a non-stick surface to roll out your icing on is particularly important when creating 'free standing lettering' as it will be seen from both sides, you don't want the back to be marked with icing sugar, especially when using coloured icing. If you are creating 'free standing lettering', rather than lettering that will be 'propped' up by another decoration, you need your icing to be at least 5mm in thickness.

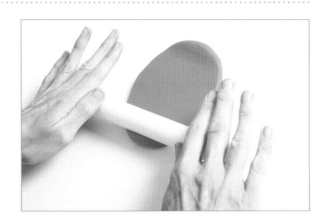

— Step 3 —

Using a very sharp craft knife, cut out your letters in your chosen font style. If you're stuck for font ideas, search on the web or under the font list when producing a letter off your computer. If you are lacking confidence when it comes to cutting out your letters, print your chosen word off and have it in front of you as a guide.

— Step 4 —

Once your letters are cut out, use your finger to smooth any rough edges, you will probably find these at any curved parts of the font as they are difficult to cut with a straight knife cleanly. Spend a few minutes smoothing each letter all over to give an immaculate finish. This is a crucial step for an impressive design.

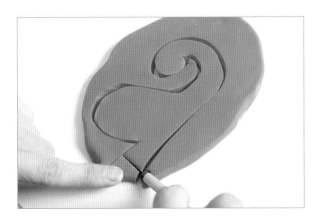

— Step 5 —

If the letters are going to be placed 'free standing' on the tier of an iced cake, rather than on the board, place one or two florist wires through each letter before drying, (see 'Wire Decorations' in the Cupcake Course). If the letter is large and heavy, use a bamboo skewer for extra support. Leave the letters overnight to dry before decorating the cake with them. Thicker lettering will need to be turned over after 24 hours and then left a further 24 hours, in order for it to thoroughly dry.

— Step 6 —

According to your design you may decorate your letters with other edible objects like sugar balls, strands, edible glitter etc using edible glue. You may want to hand paint a pattern onto them, (see 'Edible Painting' pages 50 and 51). Whichever you choose, ensure it ties in with the font or theme that you have chosen.

— Step 7 —

Once the letters are dry and decorated, add a small amount of edible glue to the base of the letter or the parts of the letter that are going to come into contact with the iced cake once positioned. Once the glue is added, position the letter and firmly hold it into position until it is fixed. With heavier letters, use Royal Icing to attach them to the iced cake as this will set like a cement, giving extra security to the fixture.

Ready to decorate!

Themed Designs

Thank you cake for
'The Royal Ballet School'

• • • • • • • • • ◆ • • • • • • • •

THE
VICTORIAN
FAIRGROUND
CAKE

• • • • • • • • ◆ • • • • • • •

Thank you cake for
The Royal Ballet School

★ ★

*" Fabulous! What a truly amazing
cake! I have never seen a cake like this;
it's a work of art. How thoughtful, it
will be enjoyed by all at The Royal
Ballet School. Thank you very much"*
- Helen Farrell, Principle Ballet Teacher,
The Royal Ballet School.

★ ★

After deciding to make a 'thank you' cake for The Royal Ballet, I began to think about the design. I really wanted to represent the 'essence' of the company through the cake, how I saw them and what they were all about. I wanted it to show my gratitude and appreciation for all the superb tuition they had given my daughter, Angel, over the past 3 years. The cake was to be presented to Angel's ballet teacher at the graduation of her associate course; it had to have the 'wow' factor, yet at the same time be graceful, elegant and classical, like the dancers themselves.

Sitting down with my sketch book, I started to make notes of the main aspects of the theme. First was 'Dancer'; tall, slim, elegant, professional. I decided my dancer would wear a lyrical style dress, the most beautiful style dress in my opinion. I drew her out in a 'poised' dance position, so she looked graceful and 'light'. I decided she would be placed at the top of the cake as my first focal point. Secondly, I thought that their logo, 'the royal crest', would be perfect as my next focal point. I asked myself, where on the cake would it look best? Will I create it 3 dimensionally or will I hand paint it? Sketching on a design sheet is a great way to generate ideas and make these sorts of decisions practically. I decided that it would be most effective to hand paint on the logo. Thirdly, as my last focal point, I wanted to create a 'tutu' as that is what most of us associate ballet with! As previously discussed in the 'Design Guide' at the beginning of the book, instead of just simply making the object out of icing, I thought 'outside of the box' and decided to incorporate just one aspect of the 'tutu' into my design, the 'frills'/netting of the skirt. I decided to position the tutu frills on the bottom tier, as I felt they looked best there as a sort of base for the rest of the design.

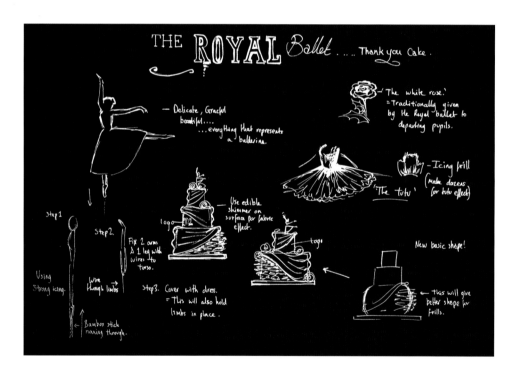

TIP: IT IS A GOOD IDEA TO HAVE AT LEAST ONE ASPECT OF YOUR DESIGN RUNNING THROUGH ALL THE TIERS SO IT LOOKS LIKE ONE WHOLE CAKE, NOT JUST 3 SEPARATE ONES...

Finally, this brought me to the rose. Traditionally each student is given a white rose upon graduation from the Royal Ballet; therefore I felt this should be an important aspect of my design. Usually, I would add colour to my designs, and I did toy with the idea of having a 'material wrap effect' around the tiers in royal blue, the colour of their uniform. However, I concluded that this would make the cake look more masculine, so to keep it elegant I decided to do a white 'material wrap effect', like the roses.

I drew out my final design with the correct colours and when I was happy with it, I began to create the cake. Follow the step by step guide below to see how! (This cake includes 2 of my signature techniques, the 'material wrap effect' and the icing 'frills' see the 'Signature Techniques' chapters for how to create them yourself.)

— *Techniques Included* —

Wrap   *Frills*   *Rose*   *Painting*

— *Preparation* —

As with all 3 tier cakes, the bottom tier must be 'strong'. For this design I used an 8" circular Chocolate Truffle cake (my own recipe, adapted so that it will take the weight of multiple tiers), you could use a fruit cake or a strong carrot cake or a mud cake (would be ideal for this small cake.)

Once the cake is cooled, carve off the edges at the base and top of the cake to create a rounded shape similar to the shape of a ball that's been squashed from above! I used a sharp bread knife to carve the cake as I find it doesn't 'pull' or 'tear' it. Hold the knife close to the cake for maximum control as the blade cuts through at a 45° angle (from the base).

After the carving is complete and the edges of the cake are as rounded as possible, cover the exterior with softened buttercream, paying particular attention to the curve at the base of the cake as you will be expecting the icing to stick to an 'under hang'.

Knead the white fondant icing to make it soft and pliable before rolling it, to prevent any cracks once it is covering the cake (see 'Icing your cake' pages 24-25). Cover the cake with the icing and use a plastic spatula to 'tuck in' the icing, sticking it firmly to the surface of the 'under hang'. Use the palm of your hand to smooth around the rounded edge at the top of the cake.

At this point I iced a 10" circular 'drum' with black fondant icing which I rolled to only 2/3mm in thickness. I always use boards of 15mm in thickness (a 'drum') with a ribbon around the base as I believe it creates a nice podium for the cake to stand on.

Prepare the silver foil surface of the board with a very small amount of edible glue, this will ensure the fondant doesn't slip whilst you are smoothing it over. As with icing a cake, roll the thin fondant onto your rolling pin, lift it off the surface and gently lower whilst unrolling it onto the cake board. Use your plastic spatula to trim off the excess icing around the edge of the board, and then smooth it with the palm of your hand for a neat finish.

Attach a black ribbon around the side of the cake board. Double sided sticky tape is perfect for holding the ribbon in place, only a few inches is needed at the back of the cake design to conceal the ends.

I decided on a black base for 2 reasons; firstly, it coordinates with the logo which I planned to paint onto the 2nd tier, creating the appearance of black-white-black-white as you look up the cake, secondly, the frills which I had planned to be placed into the bottom tier would look more dramatic against a black base.

Next, place your 1st tier iced cake onto the iced cake board, your platform and begin to prepare it for stacking by placing bamboo skewers vertically through the cake and cutting as it reaches the surface, (see 'Stacking' pages 26-27). The bottom tier is now prepared ready to take the weight of the other 2 tiers (6" and 4" circular sponges also iced with white fondant) that will need to rest on a thin cake board.

Step 1: White wrap

1. Knead a fist sized ball of white fondant icing until soft and pliable, then roll it out with a non-stick rolling pin, until it is about 5mm thick. Make sure that you apply a thin layer of icing sugar to the surface before rolling so that the icing doesn't stick. With a craft knife or a plastic spatula, cut out a large 'leaf' like shape (see 'Wrap' technique pages 34-35).

2. Gently lift the edge of the rolled out fondant which is furthest away from you and tuck under to create a rim all the way along one edge of your leaf shape. This is the first fold that gives the impression of the material wrap effect.

3. Moving from one end to the other, place your middle finger under the icing to create a ridge in the middle. Use the index finger and thumb of your other hand to accentuate and smooth over the ridge on top of the icing.

4. Repeating step 3, make a rim along the edge closest to you to create the material effect. The bottom rim should be of the same depth as the top one, the middle may be a little wider, but not too much as it may hang too far off the cake once applied to the iced surface.

5. Finally, smooth the folds of the icing with your fingers and thumb so the icing has a soft sheen appearance, like material. It is worth taking a couple of minutes to do this for a lovely finish, don't worry about the icing drying out as your constant contact with the icing surface will keep it warm, resulting in keeping it's elasticity.

Step 2: Stacking the tiers and attaching the 'wraps'

1. Place a thin foil cake board on top of the supports to take the weight of the second tier if you haven't already done so.

2. Prepare and ice with white fondant icing a 6" circular cake and then place it carefully on top of the foil board, which had been supported with the wooden dowels or bamboo skewers (see page 77). Make sure that the cake is placed centrally on top of the bottom tier. You can do this by looking down directly at the top of the stacked tier, checking to see if the spacing is equal all the way around. Take the cake off the turn table if it is too high up for you to do this.

3. Next, smear some edible glue over the surface of the icing where you wish to attach the white 'wrap' decoration. Using your finger to do this will ensure no drops or splashes of glue will go on any other part of the cake, also it will be easier for you to make sure the layer is thin an equal. Remember your hands are your best tools!

4. Holding the 'wrap' decoration gently at each end, lift and place around the glued side of the cake, slightly pulling to make sure it doesn't sag and so that it stays straight and tight to the iced surface of the cake.

5. Once you've glued the 'wrap' decoration to the side of the cake, pay attention to the ends: you want to fold them so that they give the appearance of draped material so just gently twist and mould them to how you visualise the material would rest.

6. Using your fingers, smooth the folds once more, always visualising how the icing material falling naturally.

7. Make a smaller 'wrap' to place around the opposite side of the cake, concealing the seam of the two tiers. With a smaller 'wrap', which is made for this purpose, it is possible just to create the top and bottom rims without a middle crease.

8. Using flower tools, pay attention to the ends of the 'wrap', make sure they are rounded and it looks like the icing is flowing to a point. The reason I would advise a plastic flower tool at this point, is because of its wide cone end, you can push it between the fondant folds quite far and in a more circular motion without leaving a ridge or mark in the icing.

Step 3: Frills

1. Using my 'strong' icing (see 'Frill' technique page 38), knead a ball roughly the size of your thumbnail then roll it out, keeping the edge closest to you thick and the edge furthest away from you paper thin. The 'frill' should have a 'shell' like shape.

2. Lift the icing and run your thumb along the thick edge making it slightly flat, this will enable it to stand and dry later and will also give it extra strength for when you push it into the side of the fondant iced cake.

3. Use a flower tool to press firmly along the thin edge of the icing, roll it backwards and forewords to create a frilled effect. Don't worry if you press too hard with the tool and create a rip, this will add to the effect! If you haven't got a flower tool, instead you could use the pointed end of a bamboo skewer or something similar.

4. Lift the 'frill' and fold each of the sides to create curves; try to make sure they are symmetrical but also quite deep.

5. Stand the 'frill' on the slightly flattened, thicker edge to dry. About 12 hours will be enough.

6. Repeat the process until you have at least 30 'frills'. It's always better to have more to choose from than less.

Step 4: Placing your 'frills'

When placing 'frills' into your cake design, visualise how you want the overall appearance of the cake to look, with this image in mind, start to build up the frills, every now and again stepping back to take a look, checking it looks how you want it to. There is no need for any templates, just use your imagination.

7. Apply edible glue along thick end of each 'frill', not too much as you don't want the 'frills' to sag from too much moisture!

8. Holding the sides of each 'frill', one at a time gently push them into the fondant icing on the side of the cake. Pick the smallest frills to run along the top line of the cake.

9. Repeat the process going along the edge of the cake left to right, leaving around a 2mm gap between each 'frill' so that they are not touching.

10. Create multiple rows of 'frills' until the iced area is covered. Use larger 'frills' towards the centre of the area and smaller ones again towards the bottom, this will insinuate the frilled 'tutu' effect.

11. Prepare and ice the 4" circular cake and carefully place on top. As this is a small sponge, it is light enough to not need any support on the 6" at its base.

12. Cover this tier with edible glue to prepare for the 'wrap' decoration (repeat 'wrap' technique) and then place the 'wrap' around both sides so the top tier is completely covered.

13. Make a small piece of 'wrap' icing by smoothing only one fold. A very small piece of the 'wrap' effect icing with one fold is leaving a cut flat edge on the opposite side, this helps it stand vertically.

14. Place the small 'wrap' on the top of the cake, make sure it is positioned within the circumference of the cake. This will enclose the open area at the top of the cake, making it 'full' and ready to mount any decoration.

Step 5: Roses.

"This technique of making roses uses fondant icing, which is soft and pliable therefore easy to use. It is also relatively cheap, making it a great material for trial and error. The only negative side to fondant icing is that the roses take longer to dry, however they are much quicker to make in comparison to traditional sugar craft techniques. Many ladies after attending one of my courses have said that they will never return to the traditional techniques after learning mine. When making chocolate fondant roses I use the same technique, however chocolate sets that little bit stronger than fondant icing, which is always a bonus!" (See chocolate wrap cake on page 32).

1. On a piece of folded cellophane (for example, a greetings card sleeve or an A4 plastic wallet), prepare 6 fondant icing balls into 3D teardrop shapes, and place them on the side furthest away from you. Make sure that the teardrops are spaced evenly apart.

2. Take the side of the cellophane closest to you and fold it over to create a non-stick surface on the either side of your teardrops.

3. With your index finger, press forward on each teardrop creating a 'slope'. The pointed end closest to you should remain thick so the petal has some stability. The edge furthest away should be thin like a petal. Do not press down hard on the icing, but gently smooth in a diagonal motion.

4. Select the smallest petal, hold it against your index finger and with your thumb roll the edge of the petal from right to left to create the centre of your rose.

5. Then working from the second smallest petal up to the largest, pick one up at a time and wrap around the centre.

RULES TO REMEMBER:
A. ALWAYS MAKE SURE THE TOP OF EACH PETAL LINES UP TO THE TOP OF THE CENTRE PETAL.
B. HOLD THE ROSE AT THE BOTTOM ONLY.
C. AS YOU'RE APPLYING EACH PETAL, PULL IT SLIGHTLY TO MAKE SURE IT STAYS UPRIGHT.

TIPS:
IF YOUR PETALS 'FLOP' YOU NEED TO CONCENTRATE ON RULE C.
IF YOUR ROSE SPIRALS DOWN YOU NEED TO CONCENTRATE ON RULE A.
AND IF YOUR ROSE IS VERY CLOSED UP YOU NEED TO FOLLOW RULE B MORE CLOSELY.

6. Gently curl back the edge of each petal with your index finger and thumb to create a slight point in the middle of the petal. Imagine an English rose with its soft, curled velvet like petals and simply recreate.

7. Pull off the excess icing underneath and leave the rose on the surface to dry. Do this by pushing the base of the rose onto the table.

8. Place edible glue on the back of the rose, once dry, to attach to the cake. Just a thin smear of glue will do as too much will make the rose slippery and it may fall off.

9. Always hold the rose by the centre when pushing it against the cake. The centre curl of fondant is the strongest once dry, if you try and push it into the cake by the petals they will break.

Step 6: Edible Painting.

1. Looking closely at the royal ballet logo, I begin to paint what you can see (see 'Edible Painting'), the closer you look the more accurate your image will be. Keep referring back to your image when replicating a design as you need to check everything is to scale.

Step 7: Figure

1. Using my 'strong' icing, make the base of the body around a bamboo skewer. This icing will dry quickly so keep it warm in the palm of your hand whilst moulding into shape.

2. Make the limbs for the figure on florist wires. Carefully moulding the shapes with your fingers and rolling with your hands. Insert the wire last of all with a little edible glue on the tip for when it dries within the paste.

3. Use a craft knife to sculpt the fingers and hands. A cocktail stick or the point of a bamboo skewer is also good for applying this type of detail, especially for finger nails!

4. Attach the limbs by pushing the ends of the wires through the torso, apply a little edible glue to each joint. Hold securely in place until fixed in position before letting go entirely.

Step 8: Dressing the figure

1. Using my 'strong' icing, roll out the icing for the dancers skirt, cut to shape and apply edible glue to the underside. I use the paste for this for 2 reasons: 1. Once dry it will secure the legs giving extra strength. 2. You can pull and hold the skirt to give a 'flowing' impression without it drooping and it will dry quickly in this position.

2. Place the skirt around the waist, slightly pulling it so it looks neat and tight around the torso.

3. Repeat the same process for the bodice of the dress and decorate with small icing blossoms for that feminine, decorative touch. I use a small blossom 'plunger' for this (supplied by P.M.E.) as it enables you to add delicate decorations without having to physically touch them, the plunger does that for you.

4. Use the blossom decorations to make shoulder straps for the dress, these will also help you to disguise and seal the limbs on to the torso without any obvious corrections.

5. Make a pea-size ball of fondant icing and stick on the back of the head with edible glue to create a bun hairstyle. Create the ball by rolling in the palm of your hand and then slightly flatten with your index finger while placing on the back of the head.

Step 9: Painting the figure

1. Once the bun is dry paint the hair colour all over the 'scalp' with edible paints, be sure to blend the bun and the hair together with the coloured brush strokes.

2. Paint a face on the figure, paying attention to the eyes and lips as they show expression and emotion, you decide how you want your figure to look. This also reflects how you want your viewer to feel. Is this a serious or a comedy themed cake? Set the mood with the expression!

Now you have finished! You have incorporated your practiced techniques into a themed cake, now take your knowledge and experience and design your own! Need a re-cap for your design? Refer back to the Design Guide on page 10 for inspiration and use these techniques to create your own Unique creation!

THE VICTORIAN FAIRGROUND

"This is my favourite of all my cake designs…looking at this cake I see every element of the fairground that I love, the traditional hand painted designs and the predominance of the towering Helter Skelter; it excites the child within me!"
-Danielle Gotheridge

— *Introduction* —

Once deciding on the fairground theme, I started to sketch everything that represented the fairground to me, using a selection of images I had taken while visiting the local country fair to help. I filled the page with sketches, of decorated rides, of lights, hand pained signs, a visual directory of potential decorations. I then selected 'points of interest' (see 'Design Guide').

Fairground objects are full of wonderful colours and hand painted detail, so when selecting 'points of interest' to have in my final design, I looked at the patterns on the wooden rails, the eagle on the carousel horse, the structure of the Helter Skelter and the fonts on the cake walk.

Next was the 'ideas sheet'. I looked at my selected 'points of interest' from the 'design sheet' and started to work out how I would incorporate them into the cake design. I used my imagination and sketched out several ideas, until I reached a final design. Putting all the decoration ideas together and sketching, meant that I could make decisions about where certain things would be placed, how certain colours would look together, and what sizes of individual decorations would look like on the cake as a whole. Having the final design drawn out meant that I could visualize exactly how I wanted my cake to turn out.

TIP: When creating a final design, colour is key. A design may be detailed and overwhelming but if the colours are wrong, the vision will be lost. Colours say the most about your theme and allow the viewer to recognise it instantly. For example, the fairground is a sea of strong primary and secondary colours, highlighted with gold to give that extra sparkle, so if they aren't correct you need to find out sooner rather than later!

Once I knew where everything was going to be positioned I started to think about the order each decoration would be made in. The finer decorations always must be made first; they will take the longest to dry, especially if you are planning on hand painting them. I use my 'strong' icing for these decorations as it can be rolled really thin and dries extremely quickly.

— *Techniques Included* —

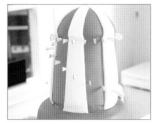

Carving

Painting

Wrap

Lettering

For this 5 tiered stacked cake, you will require at least 2 'strong' tiers, (12" and 10") for the base, the foundations for your cake, and then an 8", 6" and two 4" sponge cakes for the Helter Skelter.
The bottom 4 tiers are all iced separately in the colours decided on the design sheet.

— *Preparing to start* —

For the Helter Skelter part of the cake, use jam and buttercream to attach the two 4" sponges together to make a large sponge cylinder. With a bread knife, begin to carve the top of the cylinder to the required shape. I made an incision, starting around 15mm from the edge, and with strong, confident movements, I diagonally cut downwards towards the bottom of the tier, creating 'cone' like sides. By looking at the cakes from the front and then turning them slowly on a turn table, I could see where extra bits needed carving off to make the shape I had created symmetrical and smooth.

Once I had completed the carving, it was time to buttercream the exterior. When buttercreaming the exterior of a cake, the buttercream needs to be softened so that it doesn't tear the sides of the sponge. The best way to apply buttercream is from the base upwards, using a flexible plastic spatula.

Before icing the cylinder of buttercreamed sponge, take a 'tennis ball' size of fondant icing and mould it into a 3 dimensional semi circle, like a half of a ball. The circle base of this should be no bigger than the top of the cylinder. Place it on the top, (it will stay in place due to the sticky buttercream) and apply a thin layer of edible glue over the surface, ready for covering with red fondant icing.

Roll the kneaded red fondant icing into a long oval shape, until it is about 10mm in thickness, then lift it off the surface and cover the cylinder of sponge so that the longest sides of the oval are attached to the front and back of the cake. Trim off the sides of the icing with a spatula so that the fondant is tucked neatly around the base of the cake. The two vertical cuts along the sides may be covered later with the stripes of the Helter Skelter pattern, so don't worry about them if they end up being visible.

Finish off the sides of the icing with a plastic smoother and the dome at the top by moving the palm of your hand around it in a circular motion, smoothing out any bumps.

Finally use your index finger to define the rim under the dome of the Helter Skelter, rub it backwards and forwards until it is even all the way round.

Once all the tiers are stacked, place bamboo ready for support along with thin cake boards in-between weaker tiers, dress the base of each tier with a 15mm wide satin ribbon that colour coordinates with the design.

TIP: ALWAYS LOOK AT THE CAKE FROM EVERY ANGLE TO ENSURE EACH TIER IS PLACED CENTRALLY BEFORE FIXING IN PLACE WITH THE BAMBOO OR WOODEN DOWELING.

Firstly, you need to make the banisters for the 'cake walk' as these will take the longest to dry. Roll out the strong icing, using a small non-stick rolling pin and board.

TIP: ONLY ROLL OUT A SMALL AMOUNT OF IT AT A TIME, AS IT CAN DRY OUT VERY FAST.

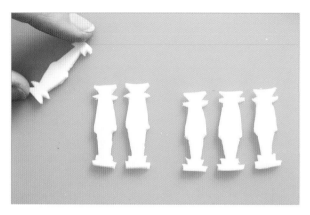

Once rolled out, use a craft knife to cut out the shape and details. Look closely at your 'design sheet' to see how the wood is carved and the proportions of the shapes. I made plenty of banister rails to make sure I had enough to go around the circumference of the tier. I took time to make sure each was the same size and shape. These are small details and are time consuming; however they will really make a difference to the overall design. The intricacies will make the viewer wonder if they are really made out of icing!

Before each banister is completely dry, (within 30 minutes of cutting out), push a 3 inch long florists wire up the bottom of each until it reaches the middle. Doing this will give them a little extra support and keep them secure when they are assembled onto the cake. Lay each banister flat to dry for at least 8 hours or alternatively over night.

When looking at the overall design, you may believe the hardest of the decorations to make is the most predominant icon of the fairground, the Helter Skelter slide and platform. I knew my biggest task would be working out the most effective way to make it from icing. I decided I would need to focus on the details and construct it in 3 parts, the slide, the platform around the top and the brackets to hold them both in place.

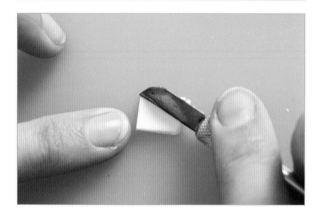

Start with the brackets. These need to be no wider than the slide, so roughly 1cm in width is sufficient, because of the strength of the icing, the bracket can get away with being very small; it should have one diagonal side so that the slide can sit perfectly in place. Use the wire technique again, so it can be pushed into the side of the cake and held securely in position.

For the platform, first, roll out the strong icing wide enough to surround the area of the Helter Skelter dome, about 1.5mm in thickness. Use a weighted object to cut around to create your circular shape, such as a saucer, or something that roughly exceeds the circumference of the dome. Then do the same for the slide which will cascade down the tier.

Remember, it is all about using your initiative to sculpt your design, to be less regimented and more creative!

Why not paint a design on the platform? Maybe old wooden floorboards or a fairground inspired pattern to give another dimension to this part of the decoration. You can use the hand painted technique to create lovely colours and patterns that really represent the fairground theme.

Once the discs are dry, use a craft knife to scrape clean the edges and give a neat finish.

Next, create the light bulbs. The image of the sparkling, colourful lights of the rides against the black sky really represents the fairground most of all to me. For these you will need some fondant icing and lots of edible glitter to make them sparkle as much as possible!

Make the bulbs the same way as you create the fondant roses. Tear pieces of fondant icing, and roll them in a circular motion in the palm of your hand, creating a fat teardrop shape, but instead of to a point, use your thumb to flatten the end and give the shape of a bulb.

Once the fondant bulbs are dry, cover them in edible glue, and then in edible glitter, gold will give you the glowing look you want!

Tip: when covering multiple small decorations in glitter, place them in a small tub or bowl, sprinkle in the glitter, put on the lid, and swirl the tub round several times for even coverage. This will also collect any unused glitter to save on wastage.

Now for the lettering, as you know with my themed cakes, when I'm using lettering I like it to be a slogan or something that represents the theme. When I was researching fairground fonts, the slogan saying 'live, laugh and love' came up often. I thought this was perfect for a celebration cake, so I chose a font style that best reflected the fairground and cut out the words from some rolled out, red, strong icing, (see 'Lettering' pages 76 and 77).

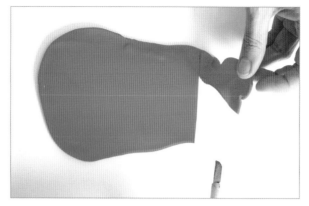

Carefully, being aware of the size and scale of each letter, drag the craft knife through the icing, following the shape of the fairground font. Each letter needs to be at least 5mm in thickness, so that once they are dry, they are strong enough to stand in front of the cake.

After leaving them overnight to dry, you can paint any detail on to your font design. Once finished, spray with a little glaze to fix any painted details so that they do not smudge.

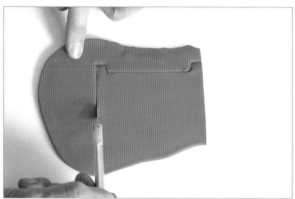

Next, make any other small fun decorations you require, to add a bit of detail to areas that will perhaps be a bit plain. Here I've chosen different sized red love hearts, made from fondant icing, to tie in with the slogan. You may want to choose stars, or even little goldfish, anything that relates to the theme!

I also made fondant icing sticks of rock, with the slogan written as if it is ran through the middle of each piece. I made these by rolling soft pink fondant icing, cutting the ends clean with a craft knife and allowing them to dry overnight, before using edible dark pink paint to create the stripes and wording. You could use different colour combinations to produce the appearance of different flavours, for example aniseed, beige and dark brown stripes, or humbug with black and white. Maybe you could match the decorations to the flavours of the cake tiers iced beneath them. There are endless small details you could add which will really give another dimension to your theme and design.

Once your cake is shaped and iced to the colour scheme decided in your final design, you have the base to start adding your decorations.

TIP: ALWAYS START AT THE TOP OF THE CAKE AND WORK YOUR ICING DOWN, THIS WAY YOU WON'T BE OVERLAPPING ANYTHING.

All two dimensional decorations need to be applied first.

Roll out some yellow fondant icing until it is around 2-3mm in thickness. Then with a plastic spatula, cut through the fondant vertically, to create several stripes for the Helter Skelter patterning. Each stripe should be about 1cm wide at the top and twice as wide at the bottom.

Using edible glue, prepare the area ready to attach the stripe decorations.

Hold each stripe carefully at the top and bottom and gently press them against the prepared glued base.

TIP: DO NOT PULL THE FONDANT STRIPES DOWNWARDS AS THIS WILL CREATE STRETCH MARKS IN THE ICING OR IT MAY RIP.

Holding it from the top and letting the strip hang will allow it to naturally fall in a vertical position. Using the side of your index finger, softly smooth the stripes under the rim of the top of the dome of the Helter Skelter, to create a ridge that the platform will go around. With your plastic spatula, tuck the bottom of the stripes neatly into the base of the Helter Skelter tier for a neat finish.

Starting at the top, begin to place your 3 dimensional decorations. I decided to represent the first of my lettering, 'LIVE', in the form of a hand painted flag, and so this is taking position top of the cake. The flag is made from strong icing, glued onto a silver florist wire and was left to dry overnight before the decorative details were hand painted on. I pushed it gently into the top of the cake.

Once all the small brackets are dry, paint them to match your cake design theme. I decided on gold with a green flat end.

Place each bracket into the cake horizontally, you need to visualise where the slide will cascade down the tier and where the circular platform will sit and position them so that they will hold them there. You might need to add a little edible glue to the 'wire end' of the bracket to give your structure that little more support.

While your brackets are settling into place, move onto the second tier down. Roll out some more yellow fondant icing, to the same thickness as before, then, using a craft knife, create the shaped stripes, as you have drawn on the design sheet. Again, these stripes are wider at the bottom, this time with an oval 'bulge' towards the top.

As with the previous stripes, prepare the surface with edible glue. Attach similar to last time, gently press the stripes against the cake, smoothing with your index finger and tidying the bottom of each with a plastic spatula.

When I looked at the painted details on the rides at the fairgrounds, I repeatedly saw these oval green and gold details. So I made some small oval discs from strong icing and painted the details on once dry. To attach, add a little edible glue in the centre of each 'bulge' and attach one small disc to each.

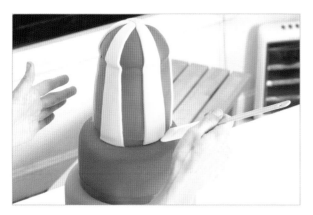

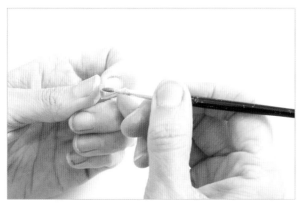
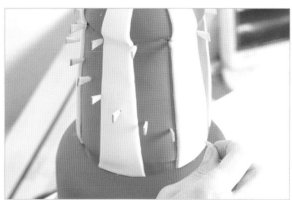

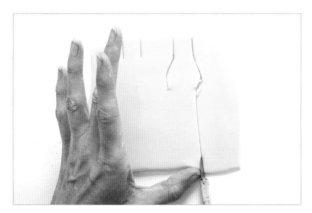

The next 3 dimensional decoration, is the red 'wrap' of icing, to create a draped material effect on the 2nd tier down. Use the 'wrap' technique to prepare your icing as shown. (see pages 28 and 29)

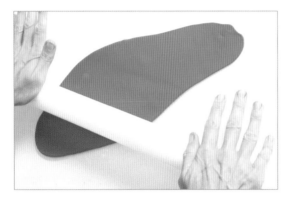

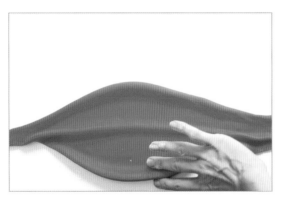
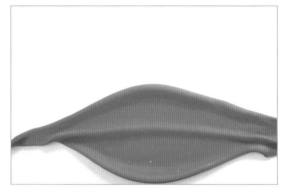

Prepare the surface where you would like to position your 'wrap' with edible glue. Picking up the 'wrap' carefully at each end, hold it against the glued surface until it is firmly attached. Then, with the ends of the 'wrap' still in your hands, tuck and fold them to give a 'ruffled' material effect ending. With the side of your hand, smooth the wrap against the cake. This will also give a nice shine to the icing.

TIP: THE SIDE OF THE PALM OF YOUR HAND STAYS AT A CONSTANT TEMPERATURE, SO IT WON'T STICK TO THE ICING WHEN SMOOTHING. IT'S ALSO PADDED, SO IS GOOD FOR MOULDING PERFECTLY AROUND ANY EDGES, GIVING A PERFECT FINISH YOU JUST CANNOT REPLICATE WITH ANY TOOL.

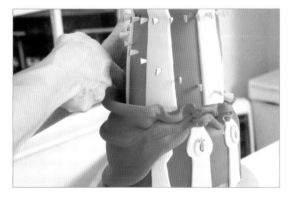 

For that extra special detail, use the gold glittery bulbs to highlight the folds of the icing material. Do this by pushing them into the soft fondant, with a little edible glue for security.

Next, move back up to the Helter Skelter tier, your brackets should be securely in place by now. Start with the platform. Before placing it on to the brackets, you will need to cut it in half, so you are left with two half circles. Use the craft knife to do this. Add a little edible glue to the top surface of the brackets and along the inner side of the platform. Then place the platform on top of the brackets and gently press each half into the fondant stripes. Press into the icing and smooth with your fingers where to two halves join, to give the appearance that the platform is in one piece. Do the same for the slide that cascades down the Helter Skelter tier. Glue and attach as before.

Now move down to the middle tier.

Apply any two dimensional decorations first to the surface of the cake. In my design, I chose to hand paint a fairground scene. This consists of all the fairground icons, for example the Big Wheel. Keeping with the colour scheme, I painted this onto the icing in gold, but used a small amount of black to create some definition within the picture. Refer to the 'Edible Painting' chapter to see how to prepare edible paints.

Once your painting is finished, spray with a little edible glaze to fix the paint, so that it does not smudge if accidentally touched.

Once you have finished all the two dimensional decorations, move onto the three dimensional ones. Add a little edible glue for security to the end of the wire of the pre-prepared icing banisters; they should be dry by now. Push each of them into the edge of the tier below, making sure they are positioned about an inch apart, until the half of the base, with the hand painted detail on it, is covered.

On the other half of the tier, away from the decoration, apply some edible glue to the surface and repeat the 'wrap' technique to finish the 3rd tier decoration.

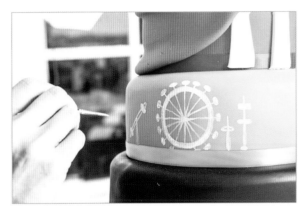

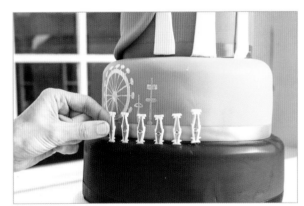

Move down to the 4th tier.

As you did with the material 'wrap' effect, roll out some red fondant icing to the same thickness as before to create some red draped, flowing curtains. Use your fingers to create curves and bumps in the curtains, to make them look more realistic. Once you have each curtain cut to size, use your eye to judge, place them against the glued surface of the black iced tier so they frame the black background. I decided that in this frame, I would paint a Punch and Judy show, as Punch and Judy, I always think, is very iconic when it comes to fairgrounds. When attaching my curtains, I made sure I left a space big enough for the edible painting.

Now it's time to add all those little extra decorations that you made earlier, taken from your sketches and designs. I created a scrolled, hand painted sign from sugar craft paste, and painted on it 'laugh' and 'cake walk'. I attached this with edible glue along with a few other decorations I had previously made.

Again, I used a red 'wrap' material effect over the sides of the black iced tier.

The red curtains are your centre point, so now can move on to the bottom tier decoration. Cut out a strip of green fondant, roughly the width of your curtain, which will be long enough to reach the end of the board. As you did with the fondant stripes on the Helter Skelter tier, add some edible glue to the surface and then gently press the strip against it, allowing it to fall and smoothing with your hands.

Use a spatula to cut off any icing that hangs over the edge of the board.

Next, make diagonal panels of different shapes and sizes out of the green fondant, to go around the rest of the base.

After cutting the rolled out fondant icing into specifically shaped strips, glue each in place, laying them flat against the cake, trimming, smoothing, and leaving to dry. Each green strip will also create extra thickness on the board, where you will be adding your letters.

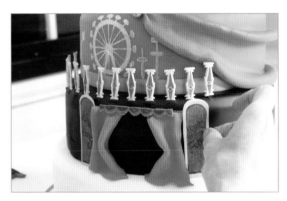

When the letters are solid and dry, and you've painted any extra decoration on them, they are ready to be placed on the cake. Add some edible glue to the underneath of the letter, place it onto the iced board and press down firmly on top of the base of the bottom.

TIP: DON'T PRESS ON THE TOP OF EACH LETTER, AS ANY EXTRA PRESSURE WILL MAKE THE LETTERS WEAK. MY STRONG ICING IS TOUGH BUT IT WILL ONLY TAKE SO MUCH.

Press into the fondant icing on the base until the letter is firmly attached to the fondant, (roughly about 10 seconds). If you can see that the letter is vertical, let go and allow it to dry. Repeat this process with each letter, using your eye to make sure each is spaced apart evenly. Once all four letters are positioned correctly and vertically, allow them to dry before moving the cake.

TIP: IF YOU FIND THAT THE LETTERS ARE WOBBLY OR UNEVEN OR IF YOUR NOT QUITE SURE ABOUT LEAVING THEM TO DRY FREESTANDING, USE SOMETHING LIKE A SKEWER, A BAMBOO STICK OR EVEN A ROUND BALL OF ICING TO PROP THEM UP AT THE BACK, FOR EXTRA SECURITY, THIS CAN ALWAYS BE REMOVED AFTER THE LETTERS HAVE DRIED.

Once everything is dry, add any finishing touches, extra decorations (hearts etc) and/or more hand painted details, to make your cake look as spectacular as possible!

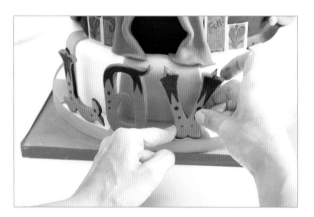

The Cupcake
Course

The cupcake course was one of my client's ideas, she said that she had read all the decorating books she could find but none of them showed decorations as unique as mine. She thought that they were all very basic and easy and there was nothing challenging for an aspiring cake designer.

I have a specifically designed course room in my shop and it is there where my clients are taught all the basic skills and techniques used to decorate larger cakes, but on a cupcake scale. I believe this widens their imagination, skills and techniques so that they are able to approach any type of cake that needs decorating for any occasion!

Another thing I aim to do through the course is produce maximum effect on a minimum budget. I begin by introducing the idea of purchasing only the primary food colours (red, yellow, blue and black) and the fact that using only them you can create an array of tones, effects and decorations. However, on my course and in the designs I am about to show you, all the cupcake decorations are made from white fondant icing and only one other colour, in this case the colour is red. It is extremely effective; there are so many contrasting designs that can be created and many different tones of pink that can be found, yet it is so simple!

The first and most important tool that you will use is your hand. The padded part to the left and right of the base of your hand called the Thenar and the Hypothenar, (see Hand Diagram page 15) can be used to smooth icing perfectly, better than any plastic smoother as you have control, you can mould your hand around the top of the cupcake, making your edges neat and professional looking. Unlike the centre of your hand, these parts generally stay at room temperature, enabling you to buff the icing to a shine, without it becoming sticky. The same applies to the smoothing of the edges of larger cakes. Again, it's about the contact you have with your materials, being in control of the appearance of your icing, using your hands makes it much easier to control how much pressure you are applying and where, creating a perfect finish.

Follow the steps of my cupcake course and create your very own gift boxes. Experiment by changing the basic colour and cutting out different shapes to create a gift box for a completely different occasion.

TIP: WHEN BAKING YOUR CUPCAKES PUT THEM IN THE LOWER HALF OF THE OVEN, THIS WILL STOP THEM RISING TOO HIGH AS WHEN BAKING CUPCAKES TO DECORATE, A FLAT, EVEN TOP IS BEST.

— Using these techniques on larger cakes —

When I originally set out the cupcake course over a couple of years ago at my first shop, the idea was always to open people's eyes to an alternative way of thinking about cake decorating. The fact we were working on cupcakes was purely because of the time we had. I didn't see the point of holding a course which involved piping some buttercream, sprinkling on a touch of edible glitter and cutting out a flower or butterfly to place on top! That wasn't the way I decorated cupcakes. It was important for me as a tutor to introduce my way of designing cupcakes and it was exactly the same way I designed all my cakes.

Theme and colour scheme is essential with a cupcake display, whether you are creating a tower of blues and whites for a baby boy's christening or a table of blacks and hot pinks for a steamy 'Hen night', make a visual statement with your colours, they should represent the occasion. On my courses I recommend using 1 colour, with either black or white. This way you will instantly have a strong contrast for your designs. Also with the techniques I show you, you will create a secondary colour (i.e. red as your primary colour with white will create pink, your secondary colour) without having to purchase another colouring. As your secondary colour has come from your primary colour, they will naturally compliment each other, following this method will eliminate 'clashing' colours. Many people will think, "I like pinks and lilacs (2 secondary colours) for my design", but they won't create a dramatic contrast and their design will be quite one dimensional.

When decorating cupcake displays for weddings and other special occasions, I always try to think about the design the same way I would if it were for the tiers of a larger cake. Would a quilted effect fit in with the style of the cake? Do I need to use decorations on wires to elevate the design, (flat cupcakes on a stand can look a little boring without something standing upright to capture the guests' attention). Could I paint something printed on their invitations onto the icing to tie in with the theme? All of these techniques are used on larger cakes and introducing them on smaller cupcakes enables my students to learn the methods quickly, opening their minds up to a different way of cake design.

— *Cupcake Course* —

Equipment:

• 6 vanilla cupcakes • White fondant icing • Red fondant icing
• Heart cutter • Edible glue • Edible glitter
• Edible gold dragee balls • Non–stick rolling pin • Plastic spatula

Fondant Roses

Get an A4 plastic wallet, cut open down the vertical side, place it landscape in front of you and open up. You will be presented with 2 A4 landscape sheets of plastic, joined at the middle.

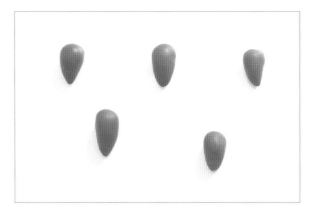

— Step 1 —

First create 5 fat tear drop shapes made from fondant icing. Do this by tearing a lump of the fondant icing and rolling it into a ball in the centre of your hand. After you have made the fondant ball, roll it up and down between your hands and pinching one side of the ball to create a teardrop shape. Repeat this another four times.

— Step 2 —

On the side of the plastic sheet that is furthest away from you, stagger the 5 tear drop shapes across it with the pointed ends closest to you. Fold the plastic sheet over the top, to create a non stick surface. Using your index finger, press down on each fondant teardrop, you want the pointed end to remain thick and the flat end furthest away from you, the edge of the petal, to be thin. You want to feel a slope from the pointed end to the thin end.

— Step 3 —

Avoid pressing in the centre because that will ruin the structure of the petal, making your roses appear floppy. Keep each petal quite strong by not over working it, smooth your index finger down towards the edge and run your finger over it to make sure its paper thin.

— Step 4 —

Once you've done this with all 5 fondant teardrops, open the plastic sheet. Start with the smallest petal and end with the largest, picking up one at a time. With the smallest petal, roll using your index finger and thumb, from one side to the other, left to right or vice versa, to form a spiral shape, this is the centre of your rose.

TIP: ALWAYS HOLD AT THE BOTTOM, THIS WAY YOUR ROSE WILL DEVELOP AND OPEN OUT NATURALLY. IF YOU DON'T HOLD IT TOWARDS THE BOTTOM YOUR ROSE WILL TURN OUT TO BE A SORT OF CONE SHAPE AND YOUR PETALS WILL STAY CLOSED AT THE TOP.

— Step 5 —

Pick up your second petal; place it against the centre petal you have just made. If you are right handed, hold it with your left hand against the back of the centre petal, with your right hand pull the petal round very gently. The reason you're pulling the fondant round, is to keep the petal vertical and in line with the other. Again, always hold at the bottom, let the rose develop and fall out naturally.

— Step 6 —

Apply each of the remaining petals in this way. Make sure each is always the same height as the centre petal, or a little bit higher. If it's not, you'll see that your rose is cascading down like a spiral. Always holding your rose at the bottom, as you apply each petal you will start to see the full rose start to form.

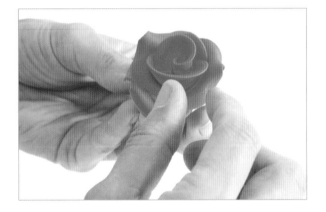

— Step 7 —

Once all petals are applied to the rose, use your index finger and thumb, working from the outside of the rose inwards, to stroke the sides of each petal back, you can also create a point in the centre, to make it look like a true English rose.

With a fondant rose you will find that the fondant will have gathered underneath. Use this to stand the rose up to dry and to go back later to when you've finished icing the rest of your cupcakes.

Marbling

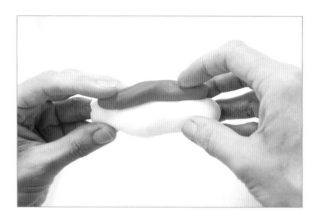

— Step 1 —

Using the left over bits of red icing from making your roses, make a fat sausage shape, and then make another from the white fondant icing you also have. Place them next to each other.

— Step 2 —

Using the tips of your fingers and thumb, to avoid sticking, twist the 2 coloured icing sausage shapes together to form a marbled pattern. By doing this you are bonding the two parts of fondant icing, as well as spiralling them together.

— Step 3 —

Twisting and folding the two fat sausages 3 times will create a nice bold pattern, 5 times will create a medium pattern, and 7 times will create a very fine pattern. I find that 3 times is sufficient for this cupcake design.

— Step 4 —

Put the ball of marbled icing down in front of you. It doesn't matter that you may have 'splits' in the ball where the icing hasn't completely moulded together, because it is soft fondant the splits will mould together once rolled.

— Step 5 —

Lightly cover your surface with icing sugar and use the non stick rolling pin to roll until the icing is about 2-3mm thick. Remember not to turn the icing over when rolling, as you don't want your pattern being spoilt by the white icing sugar clouding it.

— Step 6 —

Take your cupcake cutter and use it as a view finder, move it over the marbled icing until you find a circle with a pattern you wish to use to decorate the top of your cupcake. Cut down on the fondant icing with the cutter and place the circle on the top of your cupcake.

Always place one side down first, within the foil edge, and then continue to lay down the rest of the icing, tucking it into the foil with the side of your finger. Then smooth over around the edges and the

top with the palm of your hand, this will create a nice neat finish and a smooth iced top with no bumpy bits. With the left over icing from your marbling, knead it together to create a pink fondant. Now you have your pink icing ready for your next step and next decoration.

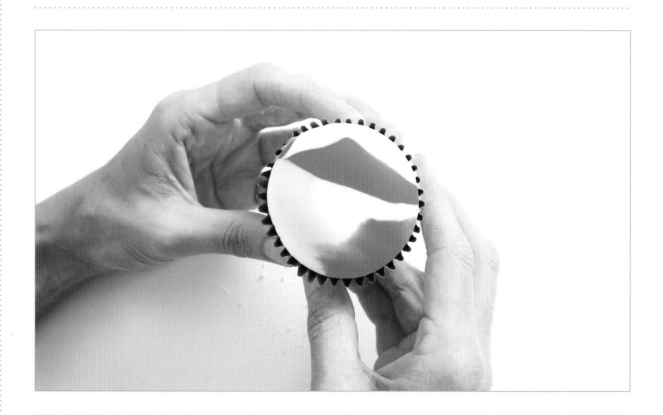

Stencilling

After rolling out your icing to around the same thickness you did for marbling, cut out a pink circle of fondant, place onto your cupcake and smooth accordingly.

— Step 1 —

For stencilling you can use a cutter, or you can use any object that creates a pattern, it can be a heart cutter, a shoe, a bow, a butterfly, anything that's going to go with the theme of your cupcakes. I am going to show you with a stiletto shoe stencil.

— Step 2 —

Place the stencil down on the top of the soft fondant icing on your cupcake, rock slightly, left to right, backwards and forwards, to make an even indentation in the surface of the icing.

— Step 3 —

Remember not to press too hard, you do not want to expose any of the sponge underneath by breaking through the icing. Once your indentation is clear, put the stencil down.

— Step 4 —

Dab your index finger gently into the edible glitter and then dab, gently again, over the top of the imprint. It doesn't need to be neat or within the lines of the imprint. You could use the tip of a soft brush, like a new make up brush, but as previously stated, I believe direct contact with your materials enables you to 'sculpt' and have more control over your design.

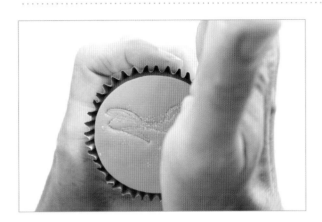

— *Step 5* —

With the palm of your hand, smooth over the top very gently, this will make sure all the glitter goes into the indentation and leave a nice glittering stencil print in the top of your cupcake.

— *Step 6* —

Hand painted messages are a nice way of adding a little extra decoration to a stencilled cupcake. Using the hand painting techniques you learned earlier, write a message, it could be for a baby shower, a hen night, a best friend or simply with love, depending on what the theme of your cupcakes is.

Now to ice your 4th cupcake pink marble.

After rolling out your icing to around the same thickness you did for marbling, cut out a pink circle of fondant, place onto your cupcake and smooth accordingly.

— Step 1 —

Use the pink that's left over from your stencil cupcake, and marble together with some more white fondant icing.

— Step 2 —

Maybe this time try to marble it 5 or 7 times, not the same as what you did before, so you now have two different types of marbled cupcakes, giving an extra dimension to your gift box.

With the left over from the pink and white marbling, again knead together to create another, this time lighter shade of pink icing ready to use to create your next cupcake design.

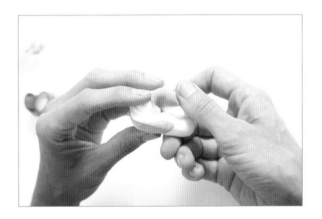

Quilting on cupcakes

— Step 1 —

Quilting on cupcakes is very similar to quilting on a large decorated cake. After kneading the icing together to create another shade of pink, roll out to the same thickness of 2-3mm and use your cupcake cutter to cut out the icing.

— Step 2 —

Again, place the icing on the top of the cupcake, first making sure the icing is tucked under on one side, then laying the rest of it down, making sure it's tucked in all the way round.

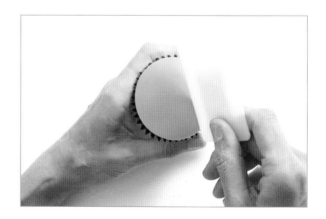

— Step 3 —

Then, using the side of your head, smooth round the edges and gently over the surface to give a perfect smooth finish. (Refer to 'Hand Diagram' page 19)

— Step 4 —

Next take your plastic spatula, and create two lines going vertically and two lines going horizontally. You could create a tighter design by applying 3 or 4 lines vertically and the same horizontally...how ever many you apply just always make sure the lines are parallel to each other.

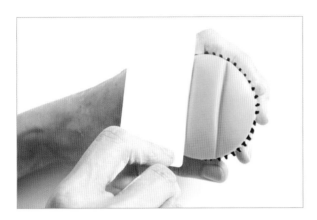

— *Step 5* —

As you gently press the spatula into the top of the cupcake, rock backwards and forwards to create an even indentation, and then gently move your spatula, left to right, to give a smoothed effect on each line.

— *Step 6* —

As the four lines cross over this creates a quilted appearance on your cupcake. Finally, use the gold edible dragee balls and place them where the lines cross, to give a perfect finish to the quilted cupcake you have created.

Wire decorations

When creating wire decorations for your cupcake, roll out your remaining pink icing, (this could be any colour that you have remaining, depending on what colour scheme your cupcakes are). It's all about using up every last bit of icing and preventing any wastage. This time, you want your icing to be rolled a little bit thinner, about 1.5mm.

— *Step 1* —

You can use any cutter you like that will go with your theme, a heart cutter, or a star; you could even have numbers to represent ages or letters for names. Alternatively, you could use a craft knife and cut out a completely different and unique shape of your own.

— *Step 2* —

Take a florist wire and dip the end of it into some edible glue. Florist wires usually come 30cm long, so it will need cutting down with a pair of scissors to about 5cm. This will enable the lid to your gift box to close without damaging the decorations.

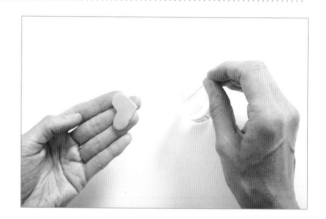

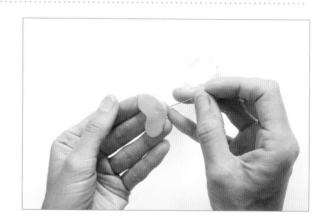

— *Step 3* —

Hold the decoration in the middle gently, between your middle finger and your thumb, and then push the wire through the bottom with the other hand. When you feel the wire underneath your thumb, you know that the wire is half way through the decoration.

— *Step 4* —

Immediately stop pushing the wire as this will leave enough space for the edible glue to dry within the icing. When cutting out your own decorations for wires, remember you do not want the weight to be much heavier than this...as gravity will make the icing fall down the wire, even after drying.

— *Step 5* —

Lay your decoration flat and allow it to dry for as long as you can. Turning the decoration over half way through the drying time will enable it to dry thoroughly.

— *Step 6* —

You could maybe decorate your wire decoration with a little bit of edible glitter, or you could use your hand painting technique to do some small extra details. Once dry, you have the perfect wire decorations, ready to go on to your cupcakes.

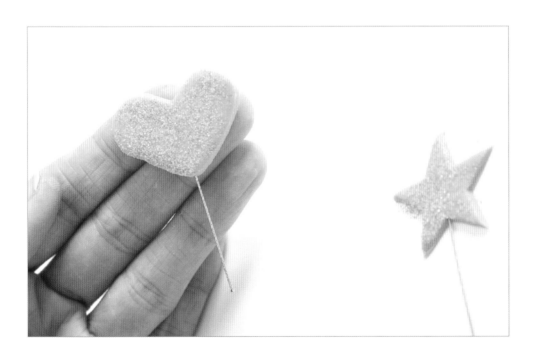

Edible painting on cupcakes

— *Step 1* —

First of all create your paint by using the dipping solution and chosen dusting powders, in your palette. When painting a rose, I like to have a variation of colours; I like to have dark colours that show the depth of the inside of the rose, and lighter colours to show the light on the edge of the petals.

— *Step 2* —

Ice a cupcake with white fondant icing, using the same techniques and smoothing as before. You want your paint to be at a consistency that is not thin and runny but not too thick and unmanageable. Look at the rose you made earlier and use this as a template to begin painting your decoration.

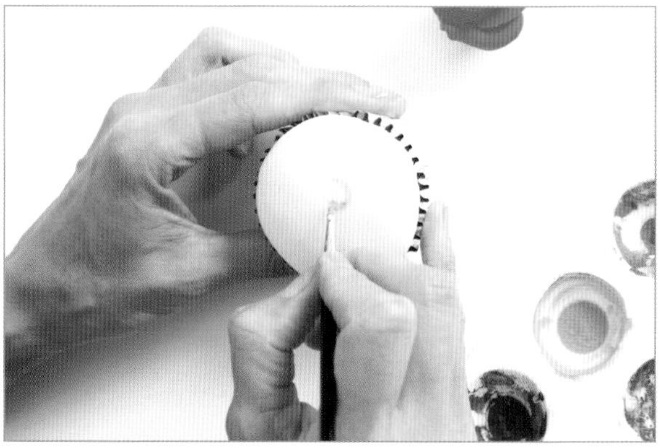

— *Step 3* —

Start by using a light colour to basically plan the outline, the lines and edges of each petal, this way if you've made a mistake you can use a darker colour to go over it and correct it.

— *Step 4* —

Once you've planned out the position of each petal, look at the rose and see where it is dark and light. Paint on the light colours where the light shines on the edge, and then go for a medium colour to fill in the main part of each petal.

— Step 5 —

Then use your darker colours, look carefully where the shade is at the base of each petal towards the centre of the rose, and fill in where you see. Remember, you are simply 'shading', as if you were colouring in a drawing of a 3 dimensional object. Think back to when you were drawing cylinders and pyramids at school, and simply apply that technique to each individual petal.

— Step 6 —

You now have a combination of light, dark and medium colours to show a realistic in depth painting of a rose. This will perfectly match your rose decoration in your gift box and give that 'something special' to the box on a whole; the receiver will title it "to good to eat!!"

Presentation.

Finally, constructing your gift box and putting the cupcakes together:

— Step 1 —

First, on the centre of a plain white iced cupcake, place a small amount of edible glue. Lift up your red fondant rose and tear off any excess fondant icing beneath it, so you are left holding the base of your rose between your index and middle fingers, making sure you're not damaging the petals.

— Step 2 —

Place the rose on top of the glue gently. Hold in position for a few seconds, until it finds its place to rest, and then allow it some time to dry. 30 minutes is sufficient enough for the fondant to bond in place, enabling you to pick the cupcake up and place in your gift box.

— Step 3 —

Next, choose a cupcake for the wire decoration to be placed on. Pick up your wire decoration, and holding it by the wire, push it into the cupcake. I have chosen a 'marbled' one for this so that the cupcake has a 3 dimensional decoration, as well as a 2 dimensional one, without either interfering with or masking one and other.

— Step 4 —

TIP: NEVER PUSH THE DECORATION IN BY HOLDING THE ICING PART; THIS MAY RESULT IN YOUR HEART TEARING AND FALLING DOWN THE WIRE.

— Step 5 —

Arrange your cupcakes inside a colour co-ordinated gift box of your choice accordingly...and you're finished!

You now have created a variation of cupcake designs, using 6 different techniques, all decorated individually. Just by using one colour which was red, mixing with your white fondant, you can create a range of different colour shades and attractive designs for any occasion or theme. Next time, try different themes and/or colours of your own, but remember each of the techniques, as they can be used widely.

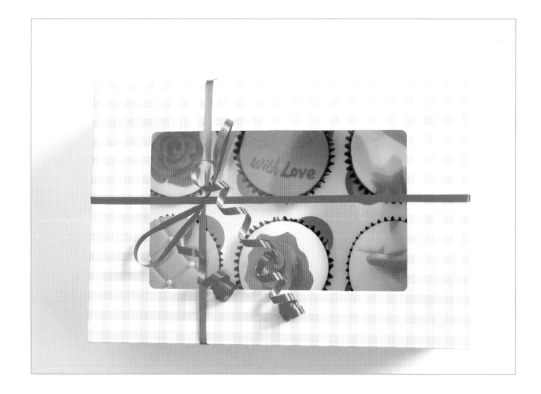

"The course was fantastic, it was so easy once you showed us how, I couldn't believe it! When I took the cupcakes home, my family didn't believe I had made them, thank you!"

- Nicola Cannon

— *Final Word* —

INTRODUCING ANY OF MY SIX SIGNATURE TECHNIQUES IN TO THE CELEBRATION CAKES YOU NOW PRODUCE, WILL BE OF AUTOMATIC ASSISTANCE TO YOUR CONFIDENCE IN CREATING THEM. BEFORE LONG, YOU WILL BE USING TWO OR THREE OF THE TECHNIQUES WITHIN YOUR OWN CAKES, ALMOST AS A SECOND NATURE, EXPANDING YOUR DESIGN CAPABILITY AND IMAGINATION.

IF YOU FIND THAT YOU'RE STRUGGLING TO THINK OF AN IDEA, ASK YOURSELF THE FOLLOWING QUESTIONS:

WHAT IS THE OCCASION? ...BIRTHDAY, WEDDING, CHRISTENING?

IS THERE A THEME? ...SUPERHEROES, GARDEN PARTY, TEDDY BEARS' PICNIC?

IS THERE A COLOUR SCHEME? ...BOLD PRIMARY COLOURS, GOLD & GLITTERY, NATURAL TONES?

WHAT IS THE SIZE? ...HOW MANY GUESTS, HOW MANY TIERS REQUIRED?

WHAT IS THE SHAPE? ...CLASSICALLY TIERED, WONKY & WACKY?

IS THERE AN INSCRIPTION NEEDED? ...PIPED MESSAGE, HAND PAINTED MOTIF, 3D FONTS?

ANSWER THOSE SIX QUESTIONS WHILST KEEPING IN MIND YOUR CLIENTS' PREFERENCES –AS SOME MAY BE LOUD AND DARING AND OTHERS MAY BE MORE TRADITIONAL AND RESERVED–; THEIR PERSONALITIES WILL AID YOUR ANSWERS. USING THE TECHNIQUES THAT YOU HAVE LEARNT WITHIN THIS BOOK WILL THEN BRING YOUR IDEAS TO LIFE.

ALWAYS REMEMBER TO SKETCH YOUR IDEAS FIRST (AS DEMONSTRATED IN THE 'DESIGN GUIDE'), BECAUSE PLANNING YOUR MATERIALS AHEAD AND COMPARING COLOUR SCHEMES WILL MAKE THE DECORATING STEPS SIMPLE, MORE ENJOYABLE AND LESS DAUNTING. NEXT IS THE CAKE CONSTRUCTION; STACKING, CARVING AND BUTTER-CREAMING ALL GIVES YOU A SOLID STRUCTURE TO BUILD UPON, AGAIN GIVING YOU A GREATER CONFIDENCE WHEN BEGINNING TO DECORATE. THEN, STEP-BY-STEP, MAKE YOUR DECORATIONS IN ORDER TO CREATE YOUR SELF DESIGNED SCULPTURE. LAST OF ALL, MAKE SURE YOU HAVE FUN! YOU ARE THE SCULPTOR, NOW GO AND FASHION YOUR VERY OWN EDIBLE ART.

I HOPE THAT HEARING AN INSIGHT TO HOW I AM INSPIRED TO CREATE MY CAKE DESIGNS HAS ENABLED YOU TO OPEN YOUR MIND TO ALL THE UNLIMITED POSSIBILITIES AND THINK OUTSIDE OF THE 'CAKE DECORATING' BOX.

OVERALL, I HOPE THAT THIS BOOK ALLOWS YOU TO BECOME A CONFIDENT CAKE DESIGNER AND TO USE YOUR IMAGINATION TO CREATE THREE DIMENSIONAL, EDIBLE ARTS IN THE FORM OF CAKES FOR FRIENDS AND FAMILY TO ENJOY WHILST CELEBRATING EACH AND EVERY UNIQUE OCCASION.

THANK YOU FOR TAKING THE TIME TO READ MY BOOK.

— Suppliers List —

For 'Strong', 'medium' & fondant icing:

Danielle Gotheridge

4 Goosegate

Hockley

Nottingham

NG1 1FF

Suppliers of products by P.M.E, Renshaws and Sugar Flair:

Culpitt Limited

Jubilee Industrial Estate

Ashington

Northumberland

NE63 8UQ

For Dusting Powders, food colouring and edible painting:

Sugar Flair Colours LTD

Brunel Road

Manor Trading Estate

Benfleet

Essex

SS7 4PS

A relaxed approach for all your photography needs:

Amy McAskell Photography

www.mcaskell.co.uk

email: amy@mcaskell.co.uk

facebook/AmyMcaskellPhotography

Graphic Design:

Pmlowther@gmail.com

— *Thank You* —

I WOULD FIRSTLY LIKE TO THANK MY CHILDREN FOR THEIR FOREVER HEART-WARMING CARE AND SUPPORT — PLUS THE ENDLESS CUPS OF TEA SUPPLIED TO ME WHILST WRITING THIS BOOK. THEY HAVE BEEN EXTREMELY PATIENT OVER THE YEARS; THROUGH ALL OF THE LATE NIGHTS I'VE HAD TO SPEND WORKING IN THE SHOP, DECORATING CAKES, CLEANING AND JUST GENERALLY PREPARING FOR THE NEXT WORKING DAY. I AM ESPECIALLY THANKFUL TO MY ELDEST DAUGHTER ROBYN, WHO HAS BEEN CONSTRUCTING AND BUILDING VARIOUS WEBSITES FOR THE BUSINESS SINCE THE AGE OF ELEVEN, KNOWING HER MOTHER'S COMPLETE IGNORANCE AND ILLITERACY OF ANYTHING TECHNICAL!

I WOULD ALSO LIKE TO THANK MY CLOSEST FRIEND, DEBORAH JEFFERY, WHO HAS BEEN MY RIGHT HAND WOMAN WHILST BUILDING THE BUSINESS TO WHERE IT IS TODAY. FOR HER LOYALTY, I AM EXTREMELY GRATEFUL.

AMY MCASKELL IS MORE LIKE A SISTER THAN A FRIEND AND WITHOUT HER PASSION FOR PHOTOGRAPHY I COULD NOT HAVE DISPLAYED THE IMAGES IN THIS BOOK. SHE HAS BEEN VERY PATIENT WHILE PREPARING AND PRODUCING ALL THE 'STEP-BY-STEP' GUIDES, GIVING HOURS, DAYS, WEEKS OF HER TIME TO SUPPORT ME ....BUT WE HAVE LAUGHED AND FOR THAT I AM FOREVER IN HER DEBT!

FINALLY, I WOULD LIKE TO THANK SUE AND PETE AT "THE FINISHING TOUCH" FOR THEIR TIME AND ENCOURAGEMENT; WITHOUT THEM, MY PASSION FOR CAKE DECORATING WOULD BE NONE EXISTENT. THEY TRULY ARE GENUINE, LOVELY PEOPLE.

THANK YOU

— *Notes* —

— *Notes* —

— *Notes* —